T. J. Hutchinson

Patriots of Salem

Roll of Honor of the Officers and Enlisted Men, During the Late Civil War,

from Salem, Mass.

T. J. Hutchinson

Patriots of Salem
Roll of Honor of the Officers and Enlisted Men, During the Late Civil War, from Salem, Mass.

ISBN/EAN: 9783337111922

Printed in Europe, USA, Canada, Australia, Japan

Cover: Foto ©ninafisch / pixelio.de

More available books at **www.hansebooks.com**

Established A. D. 1848.

STEAM

Book and Job Printing

ESTABLISHMENT.

T. J. HUTCHINSON & SON,

Respectfully announce to the public, that at their new location, in the new and spacious building

237 ESSEX STREET,

PRICE BUILDING,

COR. ESSEX & WASHINGTON STREETS,

SALEM, MASS.,

With improved and valuable machinery—abundant room—expert and careful workmen—they are prepared to execute every description of PRINTING, usually required by the MERCHANT, MANUFACTURER OR BUSINESS MAN.

Our long experience in this department of the business (having been located at the old stand for more than 27 years,) enables us to offer to our customers a quantity of work, with prices and promptness that cannot fail to satisfy. Having studied the interests of our customers, we are enabled to meet the wants of all, and with our facilities for the execution of the various branches of

Book and Job Printing,

with FAST PRESSES, ELEGANT TYPE, GOOD WORK and LOW PRICES, we hope to receive a continuance of the patronage of the public at our new location.

T. J. HUTCHINSON & SON.

Salem Publishing Company,

237 ESSEX STREET,
SALEM, MASS.

PUBLISHERS OF

SALEM, LYNN and BROCKTON
TRADES' BULLETINS,

AND

CHILD'S POCKET COMPANION AND GUIDE.

PALPH CHILDS, Manager.　　　　　　　CHAS. C. STEVENS.

Honest and judicious advertising cannot fail to bring a just reward.

ALMY, BIGELOW & WEBBER,

DEALERS IN

FOREIGN AND DOMESTIC
DRY GOODS.

LARGEST STOCK AND LOWEST PRICES.

NOS. 1, 2 & 3 WEST BLOCK,
SALEM, MASS.

OF THE

Officers and Enlisted Men,

DURING THE LATE CIVIL WAR,

FROM SALEM, MASS.,

Containing the Rank, Age, Date of Mustering in, Date of Discharge and Cause thereof, Prisoners of War, together with a list of Wounded, Killed and those who died in the service.

COMPILED WITH GREAT CARE FROM THE BEST AUTHORITIES, BY T. J. HUTCHINSON
AND RALPH CHILDS.

SALEM:
PUBLISHED BY THE SALEM PUBLISHING COMPANY.
T. J HUTCHINSON & SON, STEAM PRINTERS.
1877.

[*Entered according to Act of Congress, in the year* 1877, *by*
T. J. HUTCHINSON AND RALPH CHILDS,
in the Office of the Librarian of Congress, at Washington.]

INTRODUCTORY.

In presenting this volume to the public, the publishers have endeavored, to obtain the names of all those of our fellow-citizens, who enlisted into the service of the United States, from the city of Salem, from the commencement of the War, in 1861, to its close in 1865; and to condense the matter into a neat and compact form, for future reference, at the same time to make its cost as reasonable in price as possible, so as to bring it within the means of all who may desire to obtain a copy, as a memorial of the gallant men who risked their lives for our common country.

The number of enlistments in the Army and Navy, from Salem, from the breaking out of the war in 1861, to its close in April, 1865, was over three thousand men, and we have been enabled to obtain the names of them all, with but few exceptions. The number engaged in the Army was about twenty-eight hundred, and the Navy three hundred and eighty-five, of whom one hundred and thirteen were wounded, seventy-five killed, and one hundred and fifty-five who died of disease contracted while in the service. Forty-seven of the above were taken prisoners of war, and confined in Rebel Prisons. The whole being compiled under different headings, showing in a concise form the various departments in which our citizens were engaged, thus making a record worthy of being laid up in the archives of every household, that the children's children may celebrate, with joy and gratitude the restoration of peace, harmony and union throughout the land.

When we consider that from the State of Massachusetts, the total number of officers and enlisted men was 111,681, from which number there were 3,538 killed, 1,926 wounded, 5,671 died of disease, and 1,843 died in rebel prisons, to say nothing of the various other casualties that take place under such circumstances, it seems as if there could be hardly a family in the State that has not furnished a member to the ranks, or that has failed to contribute liberally of its substance to their support and comfort when in the field.

Massachusetts actually furnished more men to the war than were found in any one year in the State liable to military duty. With these facts before us, we have undertaken the task of collecting the names of those noble men from Salem, who were so prompt in answering the call of our common country; and went forth to deeds which will be forever cherished in the spirit, the heart, and conscience of her citizens, in the presence of their success. The irrepressible joy of a people delivered, after years of stern work and patient waiting, from the burden, almost too heavy for mortal shoulders to bear, tempered, as it was, by the tenderest sympathy for the families of the fallen, and a solemn turning to give glory and thanks, with full hearts to that God who giveth victory and healeth wounded spirits, rank among the most noble, the most sublime pieces of history of the century in which we are living.

By compiling the names of such as gave their time, their health, even their lives, if need be, to their country, there is no good reason, it seems to us, why their names should not be classed together in such a form, that coming generations may know who those heroes were. We are aware that the task is no easy matter, but have buckled on our armor to the duty, and with the assistance of kind friends have been enabled to make a list as full and complete as possible.

In the hopeful words of Mr. Seward, in his annual address, at Auburn, he said, "Death has removed his victim; liberty has crowned her heroes; humanity has crowned her martyrs; the sick and the stricken are cured—the surviving combatants are fraternizing—and the country, the object of our just pride and lawful affections, once more stands collected and composed, firmer, stronger, and more majestic than ever before, without cause of dangerous discontent at home, and without an enemy in the world."

In conclusion, the publishers take this method of returning thanks to those who have so kindly assisted them in the complicated task of collecting and correcting the lists of names herein contained, which has required months of assiduous labor, and correspondence, we now send it forth to our citizens, hoping it may prove to them that satisfaction it has to the

PUBLISHERS.

CONTENTS.

	Page
5th Regiment Infantry, M.V.M.,—three months, ...	10 & 96
8th Regiment Infantry, " "	11
13th Unattached Co. Infantry,—90 days, ...	12
5th Regiment Infantry, M. V. M.,—100 days, ...	15
16th Regiment Infantry, " "	101
Salem Cadets, " "	15
2d Unattached Co. Infantry, M. V. M.—100 days, ...	101
7th Regiment Infantry, " 6 months, ...	17
5th Regiment Infantry, " 9 months, ...	18 & 101
8th Regiment Infantry, " "	102
42d Regiment Infantry, " "	102
44th Regiment Infantry, " "	102
47th Regiment Infantry, " "	102
48th Regiment Infantry, " "	18
50th Regiment Infantry, " "	102
53d Regiment Infantry, " "	103
27th Unattached Co. Infantry,—one year, ...	103
4th Battery, Light Artillery, —M. V., three years.	23 & 97
5th Battery, Light Artillery,—M. V., "	25 & 99
8th Battery, Light Infantry,—M. V., "	99
9th Battery, Light Artillery,—M. V., "	100
12th Battery, Light Artillery,—M. V., "	100
13th Battery, Light Artillery,—M. V., "	25
14th Battery, Light Artillery,—M. V., "	100
15th Battery, Light Artillery, M. V, "	100
1st Regiment Heavy Artillery,—M. V., 3 years originally 14th Infantry,	26 & 95
2d Regiment Heavy Artillery,—M. V., 3 years,	39 & 96
3d Regiment Heavy Artillery,—M. V., originally the 3d, 6th, 7th, 8th, 9th, 10th, 11th, 12th, 13th, 14th, 15th, & 16th Unattached Co's Heavy Art.,	35 & 97
4th Regiment Heavy Artillery,—M. V. 1 year, originally the 17th, 18th, 19th 20th, 21st, 22d, 23d, 24th, 25th, 26th, 27th, & 28th Unattached Co's. Heavy Artillery, ...	37 & 98
29th Unattached Co. Heavy Artillery—M. V., one year . . .	38
1st Battalion, Heavy Artillery,—M. V., 3 years originally the 1st, 2d, 4th, & 5th Unattached Co's Heavy Art., & Co's E. & F., new organizations,	39 & 99
1st Regiment of Cavalry,—M. V., three years, ...	41 & 100
2d Regiment of Cavalry, " "	42 & 101
3d Regiment of Cavalry, " "	44
4th Regiment of Cavalry, " "	44 & 101
5th Regiment of Cavalry, " "	47
1st Battalion Frontier Cavalry,—M. V., three years, ...	47
1st Regiment Infantry, " "	48
2d Regiment Infantry, " "	49 & 103
9th Regiment Infantry, " "	52 & 103

CONTENTS.

	Page.
11th Regiment Infantry,—M.V.M., three years,	56 & 104
12th Regiment Infantry, " "	58 & 105
13th Regiment Infantry, " "	106
15th Regiment Infantry, " "	59
16th Regiment Infantry, " "	59
17th Regiment Infantry, " "	60 & 106
18th Regiment Infantry, " "	62
19th Regiment Infantry,—M. V., three years,	62 & 107
20th Regiment Infantry,—M. V., three years,	66 & 107
21st Regiment Infantry, " "	108
22d Regiment Infantry, " "	68
23d Regiment Infantry, " "	69 & 108
24th Regiment Infantry, " "	75 & 108
25th Regiment Infantry, " "	109
26th Regiment Infantry, " "	77
27th Regiment Infantry, " "	109
28th Regiment Infantry,—M. V., three years,	77 & 109
29th Regiment Infantry, " "	78 & 109
30th Regiment Infantry, " "	79
32d Regiment Infantry, " "	80 & 110
33d Regiment Infantry, " "	110
35th Regiment Infantry, " "	82 & 110
39th Regiment Infantry, " "	82 & 110
40th Regiment Infantry, " "	83 & 110
54th Regiment Infantry, " "	85
55th Regiment Infantry, " "	86
56th Regiment Infantry, " "	86
57th Regiment Infantry, " "	87
59th Regiment Infantry, " "	88
61st Regiment Infantry, " "	90
62d Regiment Infantry, " "	91
1st Company Sharpshooters,—M. V, three years,	92
2d Company Sharpshooters, " "	93
Veteran Reserve Corps,	93
Regular Army,	94
U. S. Veteran Vols., (Hancock's Corps.),	94
U. S. Colored Troops	94
Residents of Salem who enlisted in other places,	111
Officers and Seamen in Naval Service,	112
List of wounded while in service,	117
Prisoners of War,	119
List of the Killed	122
List of those who Died in service,	124

Fifth Regiment Infantry, M.V.M.—Three Months.

Company A.

NAMES AND RANK.	AGE.	DATE OF MUSTER.	TERMINATION OF SERVICE, &c.
George H. Peirson, Capt. Lieut. Col. July 5, 1861.	45	May 1, 1861	Expiration of service July 31, 1861.
Edward H. Staten, 1st Lieut. Capt. July 6, 1861.	29	"	"
Lewis E. Wentworth, 2d Lieut. 1st Lieut. July 6, 1861.	38	"	"
Charles Stiles, 1st Sergt. 2d Lieut. July 6, 1861.	25	"	"
Benj. K. Brown, Sergt.	28	"	"
Albert J. Lowd, "	21	"	"
Joseph M. Parsons, Corp.	21	"	"
John F. Clark, "	28	"	"
PRIVATES.			
Adams Charles P.	23	"	"
Buxton George B.	18	"	Disability—June 12, 1861.
Buxton George F.	22	"	Expiration of service, July 31, 1861.
Cate Samuel A.	20	"	Prisoner, July 21, 1861, exch. 1862.
Chipman Charles G.	21	"	Expiration of service, July 31, 1861.
Clemons Willam H.	20	"	"
Daniels John B.	30	"	"
Davenport Davis	20	"	"
Davidson Henry	19	"	"
Davis Charles W.	21	"	"
Dodge Charles W.	23	"	"
Dominick Joseph	21	"	"
Dowst Joshua W.	24	"	"
Drown William P.	23	"	"
Ford John F.	24	"	"
Gardner Abel	24	"	"
Gardner Charles W.	18	"	"
Gardner William H.	21	"	"
Giles Charles H.	18	"	"
Gilman John T.	19	"	"
Glidden Joseph H.	20	"	"
Gwinn Charles H.	25	"	"
Hurd William H.	30	"	"
Kehew John H.	26	"	"
Leavitt Israel P.	28	"	Disability—June 8, 1861,.
Leonard James	21	"	Expiration of service, July 31, 1861.
Libby Henry	23	"	"
Mansfield John R.	40	"	"
Maxfield James jr.	23	"	"
Melcher Levi L.	27	"	"
Morse George W.	22	"	"
Moses John H.	18	"	"
Munroe Stephen N.	27	"	"
Nimblet Benjamin F.	29	"	"
Osborne John H.	18	"	"
Osborne Laban S.	20	"	"
Palmer William H.	20	"	"
Patten James M.	18	"	"
Peabody William M.	19	"	"

10   PATRIOTS OF SALEM.

NAMES AND RANK.	AGE.	DATE OF MUSTER.	TERMINATION OF SERVICE, &C.
Perry Henry W. - - -	40	May 1, 1861	Expiration of service July 31, 1861.
Pousland John H. - - -	20	"	"
Pratt Calvin L. - - -	19	"	"
Pratt Lewis R. - - -	21	"	"
Rix Asa W. S. - - -	20	"	"
Semons Francis A. - - -	23	"	"
Sloper William A. - - -	23	"	"
Smith Henry J. - - -	22	"	"
Symonds Nathaniel A. - -	26	"	"
Tufts Rufus W. - - -	20	"	"
Warren Edward J. - - -	27	"	"
Weeks William H. - - -	22	"	"
West George - - -	27	"	"
Wheeler Samuel B. - - -	23	"	"
Williams Charles A. - -	20	"	"

Company H.

	AGE.	DATE OF MUSTER.	TERMINATION OF SERVICE, &C.
Henry F. Danforth, Capt. -	24	May 1, 1861	Expiration of service July 31, 1861.
George S. Peach, 1st Sergt. -	22	"	"
Benjamin F. Pickering, Sergt. -	37	"	"
John Pollock, "	21	"	"
Joseph B. Nay, "	19	"	"
Elbridge H. Guilford, Corp. -	19	"	"
Peter A. Ramsdell " -	24	"	"
Joseph Anthony, Musician.	21	"	"
PRIVATES.			
Berg William R. - -	27	"	Missing, returned to Mass. Aug. 1, '61.
Brown George A. - -	25	"	Expiration of service, July 31, '61.
Bulger James - -	20	"	"
Clark Edward A. - -	32	"	"
Clark Sylvester - -	20	"	"
Dow George W. - -	30	"	Prisoner, July 29, '61, disch. '62.
Eaton Alpheus - -	21	"	Expiration of service, July 31, '61.
Edwards John L. - -	26	"	"
Farrell William - -	21	"	"
Ferguson Samuel A. - -	21	"	"
Glover James jr. - -	20	"	Disability—June 29, '61.
Hackett Harrison -	21	"	Expiration of service, July 31, '61.
Hibbard Curtis A. -	24	"	"
Hoyt John A. - -	28	"	"
Kehew Francis A. -	25	"	"
Kehew George - -	19	"	"
Kimball William L. -	28	"	"
Leach Harris - -	24	"	"
Linehan Dennis - -	19	"	"
McDuffie Hugh - -	26	"	"
McFarland Charles -	23	"	"
Parsons Cyrus - -	41	"	"
Peach William jr. -	20	"	"
Perkins Joseph H. -	30	"	"

PATRIOTS OF SALEM.   11

NAMES AND RANK.	AGE.	DATE OF MUSTER.	TERMINATION OF SERVICE, &C.
Quinn John	24	May 1, 1861	Expiration of service, July 31, '61.
Shanley William	19	"	Prisoner, July 23, '61, disch. '62.
Teague William H.	23	"	Expiration of service, July 31, '61.
Thompson George A.	20	"	Killed at Bull Run, Va., July 21, '61.
Trask Henry	19	"	Expiration of service, July 31, '61.
White Henry F.	21	"	" "
White Thomas	22	"	" "
Williams William D.	21	"	" "
Wilson Jacob H.	25	"	" "

Eighth Regiment Infantry M.V.M,—Three Months

Company H.

Tibbetts George F.	23	Apr. 30, '61.	Expiration of service, Aug. 1, '61.

Company I.

Arthur F. Devereux, Capt.	25	May 18, '61	Expiration of service, Aug. 1, '61.
George F. Austin, 1st Lieut.	22	"	" "
Ethan A. P. Brewster, 2d Lieut.	23	"	" "
George D. Putnam, 3d Lieut.	26	"	" "
Charles U. Devereux, 1st Sergt.	23	"	" "
George W. Batchelder, Sergt.	23	"	" "
George C. Gray, Sergt.	25	"	" "
Charles S. Emmerton, Sergt.	18	"	" "
Alvan A. Evans, Corp.	20	"	" "
Charles F. Williams jr.	19	"	" "
John P. Reynolds jr.	21	"	" "

PRIVATES.

Archer George N.	21	"	" "
Batchelder Charles J.	25	"	" "
Brooks Joseph H.	21	"	" "
Brown Albert W.	20	"	" "
Brown Elbridge K.	21	"	" "
Carlton John W.	28	"	" "
Chapple William F.	35	"	" "
Claflin William H.	37	"	" "
Dalrymple Simon O.	22	"	" "
Dearborn Charles A. jr.	19	"	" "
Derby Putnam T. jr.	24	"	" "
Devereux John F.	26	"	" "
Dimon Charles A. R.	20	"	" "
Douglass Albert C.	24	"	" "
Field Joseph W.	23	May 18, '61.	" "
Fowler William T.	35	June 18, '61.	" "
Hale Henry A.	21	"	" "
Hall Edward A.	18	"	" "

PATRIOTS OF SALEM.

NAMES AND RANK.	AGE.	DATE OF MUSTER.	TERMINATION OF SERVICE, &C.
Hitchings Abijah F.	19	May 18, '61	Expiration of service, Aug. 1, '61.
Hodges John jr.	20	"	"
Howard Frank C.	23	"	"
Lakeman John R.	18	"	"
Luscomb Charles P.	22	"	"
Luscomb George W.	27	"	"
Mansfield Charles H.	21	"	"
Moody Converse	23	"	"
Nichols James W.	19	"	"
Osgood Edward T.	21	"	"
Palmer William L.	22	"	"
Perkins Joseph A.	21	"	"
Pratt Edwin F.	20	June 19, '61.	"
Reeves Robert W.	19	May 18, '61.	"
Ross J. Perrin	20	"	"
Ross W. H.	26	"	"
Shaw Cyrus P.	20	"	"
Smith Albert P.	19	"	"
Smith Frederick W.	24	"	"
Smith Samuel H.	20	"	"
Stevens Edward P.	36	"	Disability—July 21, '61.
Stevens George O.	25	"	Expiration of service, Aug. 1, '61.
Stimpson Edward S.	24	"	"
Swasey William R.	21	"	"
Sweetland Alonzo	26	"	"
Upton William B.	23	"	"
Ward J. Langdon	19	"	"
Whitney Charles E.	19	"	"

THIRTEENTH UNATTACHED COMPANY INFANTRY,—NINETY DAYS.

Robert W. Reeves, Capt.	22	May 16, '64.	Expiration of service, Aug. 15, '64.
George O. Stevens, 1st Lieut.	27	"	"
John W. Evans, 2d Lieut.	22	July 19, '64	"
Augustus Brown, 1st Sergt.	21	May 16, '63.	"
George H. Blinn, Sergt	23	"	"
Lebbeus Leach jr. "	24	"	"
George A. Nichols, "	18	"	"
John F. Watson, "	23	"	"
Hersey D. Pickman, Corp.	20	"	"
William G. Hammond, "	22	"	"
Albert E. Newton "	26	"	"
Andrew G. Peterson "	21	"	"
Charles Perkins "	21	"	"
Joseph W. Sanborn "	19	"	"
William H. Carter "	23	"	"
John F. Estes, Musician	18	"	"
Edward Stillman, "	18	"	"
PRIVATES.			
Austin Everett E.	20	"	"
Barry John		"	"
Bennett George A.	20	"	"
Boyce Henry	18	"	"
Brown Frederick C.	18	"	"

PATRIOTS OF SALEM. 13

NAMES AND RANK.	AGE.	DATE OF MUSTER.	TERMINATION OF SERVICE, &c.
Carroll Charles	19	May 16, '64	Expiration of service, Aug. 15, '64.
Casey David	18	"	"
Cashron John	18	"	"
Chitman William H.	18	"	"
Collins Edward A.	24	"	"
Cook David	18	"	"
Conway James	18	"	"
Cousins Joseph H.	22	"	"
Daley Patrick	20	"	"
Dalrymple George W.	19	"	"
Dwinell William P.	20	"	"
Eagan Richard J.	18	"	"
Galivan Michael	18	"	"
Green Thomas	21	"	"
Grimes Israel W	32	"	"
Griifen Henry	18	"	"
Hatch Thomas C.	18	"	"
Johnson Alfred	19	"	"
Kezar Alonzo	19	"	"
Knapp Samuel W.	20	"	"
Lagrange Charles E.	18	"	"
Lamson George A.	18	"	"
Lander William T.	18	"	"
Linehan Cornelius J.	18	"	"
Marr Michael	19	"	"
McCommie John	21	"	"
McDonnell John	18	"	"
McDonnell Philip	18	"	"
Merrill William R.	18	"	"
Moran Nathaniel	19	"	"
Murphy William	18	"	"
O'Brien James	18	"	"
Osborn William E.	19	"	"
Perkins Henry	19	"	"
Redman John	18	"	"
Smith John F.	18	"	"
Soley Frank	19	"	"
Trask James E.	21	"	"

Fifth Regiment Infantry. — One Hundred Days.

Company A.

George H. Peirson, Col.	48	July 28, '64	Expiration of service, Nov. 16, '64.
PRIVATE.			
Williams Henry	20	July 23, '64	Re-enlisted 39th Reg. Sept. 19, '64.

Company C.

NAMES AND RANK.	AGE.	DATE OF MUSTER.	TERMINATION OF SERVICE, &C.
PRIVATES.			
Hall William H.	23	July 23, '64	Expiration of service, Nov. 16, '64.
Johnson Frank E.	19	"	"
Meek Henry M.	20	"	"
Perry William A.	18	"	"
Symonds Charles A.	18	"	"
Welch W. P.	29	"	"

Company H.

William H. Archer, Corp.	22	July 20, '64.	Expiration of service, Nov. 16, '64.

Company I.

NAMES AND RANK.	AGE.	DATE OF MUSTER.	TERMINATION OF SERVICE, &C.
Edward H. Staten, Capt.	31	July 15, '64	Expiration of service, Oct. 27, '64.
Joseph H. Glidden, 1st Lieut.	23	"	"
Robert P. Clough, 1st Sergt.	40	"	"
Joshua W. Dowst, Sergt.	27	"	"
Benjamin F. Pickering "	40	"	"
Charles A. Williams "	23	"	"
Charles H. Gwinn "	27	"	"
Nathaniel A. Symonds, Corp.	29	"	"
John Chandler, "	36	"	"
Daniel Staniford "	27	"	"
Joseph E. Waldron "	23	"	Re-enlisted, 3d Regt. H. Art. Oct. 6, '64.
PRIVATES.			
Adams Peter F.	30	"	Expiration of service, Oct. 27, '64.
Adams Thomas M.	22	"	"
Burding Edward W.	18	"	"
Dodge Joseph H.	18	"	Died, Sept. 5, '64, Fort Delaware.
English James W.	25	"	Expiration of service, Oct. 27, '64.
Evans George	20	"	"
Flood John	18	"	"
Goodrich William	20	"	"
Goss George L.	21	"	"
Hall James A.	18	"	"
Hines Thomas T.	18	"	"
Howard David A.		"	Deserted, July 17, '64, Readville, Mass.
Howard Nathaniel K.	20	"	Expiration of service, Oct. 27, '64.
Lamb Hiram O.	23	"	"

NAMES AND RANK.	AGE.	DATE OF MUSTER.	TERMINATION OF SERVICE, &c.
Lord Charles L.	26	July 15, '64	Expiration of service, Oct. 27,'64.
Lord George C.	28	"	"
Manning Philip A.	19	"	"
Moulton Charles E.	21	"	"
Nichols William H. jr.	19	"	"
O'Connor John	19	"	"
Oldson Joseph H.	20	"	"
Paine Charles D.	21	"	"
Pettengill George	40	"	"
Rider Joshua O.	28	"	"
Rogers John E.	19	"	"
Rowley Robert	26	"	"
Sheehan John J.	18	"	"
Stevens Samuel A.	20	"	"
Stone George L.	20	"	"
Thomas Joseph F.	18	"	"

Salem Cadets, M.V.M — One Hundred Days

	AGE	DATE	TERMINATION
John Louis Marks, Major	40	May 26, '62	Expiration of service, Oct. 11, '62.
Joseph A. Dalton, Capt.	47	"	Major 40th Reg. Inf. Aug. 20, '62.
Richard Skinner jr., 1st Lieut.	43	"	Expiration of service, Oct. 11, '62.
John Pickering jr., Adjt.	42	"	"
Joseph C. Foster, 2d Lieut.	32	"	"
Thomas H. Johnson 2d Lieut.	28	"	"
Jonathan A. Kenney, 2d Lieut.	49	"	"
A. Parker Browne, 1st Sergt	26	"	Adjt 40th Reg. Inf. Sept. 5, '62.
Edward A. Simonds, 1st Sergt	38	"	Expiration of service, Oct. 11, '62.
George C. Bancroft, Sergt.	24	"	2d Lt. 40th Reg. Inf. Aug. 22, '62.
Charles H. Dalton, "	26	"	Expiration of service, Oct. 11, '62.
George D. Glover, "	38	"	"
Edwin R. Hill, "	35	"	"
Charles H. Pinkham "	39	"	"
Charles W. Ashby "	31	"	"
Isaac P. Foster jr "	35	"	"
Philip G. Skinner "	29	"	"
Ephraim A. Annable, Corp.	21	"	"
Servington S. Burnett "	25	"	"
Warren P. Davis "	37	"	"
Henry W. Downing "	23	"	"
Charles E. Getchell "	22	"	"
Daniel E. Leach "	27	"	"
Robert McCloy "	23	"	"
Nathaniel A. Robbins "	23	"	"
Albert L. Towle "	23	"	"
John B. Browne, Musician.	15	June 16, '64	"
Edward Stillman "	15	"	"
PRIVATES.			
Austin Alden K.	20	May 26, '62	"
Barenson Abram F.	20	"	"
Barker Charles F.	20	June 6, '62	"
Bennett Abram E.	20	May 26, '62	"
Brown Samuel A.	18	June 4, '62	"

NAMES AND RANK.	AGE.	DATE OF MUSTER.	TERMINATION OF SERVICE, &c.
Buffum Charles C.	31	May 26, '62.	Expiration of service, Oct. 11, '62.
Buxton George E.	23	"	" "
Caswell George A.	18	June 4, '62.	" "
Chamberlain Luther L.	30	May 26, '62.	" "
Clough Robert P.	41	June 4, '62.	" "
Colman Benjamin F.	27	May 26, '62.	" "
Collins Edward jr	23	"	" "
Copeland George A.	18	June 4, '62.	" "
Cutts Benjamin	20	May 26, '62.	" "
Cutts Richard A.	21	"	" "
Dalton William T.	31	"	" "
Dodge Charles P. jr.	21	"	" "
Foster William J.	26	"	" "
Gardner Charles W.	19	June 4, '62.	" "
Gardner Joseph D.	26	May 26, '62.	" "
Gardner William D.	20	"	" "
Glazier George W.	23	"	" "
Goldthwaite George C.	30	"	" "
Goodhue Hiram	21	"	" "
Grant Benjamin H.	26	"	" "
Griffin Eben jr.	26	"	" "
Haskell Edward B.	26	"	" "
Henfield Joseph H.	22	"	" "
Higbee Stephen D.	32	"	" "
Kezar Charles H.	24	"	" "
Kilham William G.	28	"	" "
Kimball Charles A.	30	"	" "
Kimball George S.	25	"	" "
Lamb Hiram O.	22	"	" "
Littlefield Elmer	23	"	" "
Lord Charles L.	23	June 4, '62.	" "
Lord Francis	32	May 26, '62.	" "
Loud David jr	30	"	" "
Loud Joseph G.	29	"	" "
Maloon William H.	18	"	Disability, Aug. 18, '62.
Mansfield Daniel R.	18	June 4, '62.	Expiration of service, Oct. 11, '62.
Marshall Ezekiel H.	28	May 26, '62.	" "
Merrill John C.	25	"	" "
Millett Charles 2d	33	June 4, '62.	" "
Millett William H.	25	May 26, '62.	" "
Mitchell Edward	24	June 4, '62.	" "
Perkins Joseph A.	21	" 6	" "
Pickering Benjamin P.	19	May 26, '62.	" "
Prince William W.	27	"	" "
Pousland David N.	19	"	" "
Radford George A.	20	"	" "
Remon John C.	32	June 6, '62.	" "
Ricker Francis M.	18	May 26, '62.	" "
Staniford Daniel	20	June 6, '62.	" "
Stillman Amos	19	"	" "
Stocker Charles H.	18	May 26, '62.	" "
Symonds George H.	23	"	" "
Tucker Horace	20	"	" "
Tyler Alfred	20	"	" "
Upham Oliver W. H.	19	"	" "
Upton Daniel	25	"	" "
Very Nathaniel O.	24	"	" "
Waldron Joseph E.	22	"	" "
Webb John F.	19	"	" "
Wills George A.	24	"	" "
Whitmore William W.	39	June 4, '62.	" "
Wiggin George F.	41	" 7,	" "
Yasinski Edmund A.	27	May 26, '62.	" "

Seventh Regiment Infantry, M V.M.—Six Months.

Company B.

NAMES AND RANK.	AGE.	DATE OF MUSTER.	TERMINATION OF SERVICE, &C.
Edward H. Staten, Capt.	30	July 1, '62	Expiration of service, Dec. 31, '62.
Isaac S. Noyes, 1st Lieut.	31	"	"
Joseph M. Parsons, 2d Lieut.	23	"	"
Joseph H. Glidden, 1st Sergt.	21	"	"
James Leonard, Sergt.	22	"	"
Henry Libby, "	24	"	"
Chas. H. Phippen, "	23	"	"
Francis A. Semons, Corp.	24	"	"
Benj. F. Pickering, "	38	"	"
Chas H. Gwinn, "	25	"	"
Sidney B. Rowell, "	21	"	"
Thomas A. Rowell, "	23	"	"
John Gardner, Musician.	53	"	"
Rupart J. Chute, "	15	"	"
PRIVATES.			
Babcock John H.	28	"	"
Bassett John A.	22	"	"
Bell William H.	18	"	"
Bousley George E.	22	"	"
Brown Albert W.	21	"	"
Brown John B.	15	Oct. 22, '62.	"
Carr W. H.	21	July 1, '62	"
Carter William H.	18	"	"
Chandler George A.	21	"	Disability—Oct. 9, '62.
Chase Benjamin E.	38	"	Expiration of service, Dec. 31, '62.
Cheney Joseph H.	31	"	"
Chute Isaiah	39	"	"
Donahoe Patrick F.	17	"	"
Easterbe Thomas W.	34	"	"
Fowler Newton G.	36	"	"
Fullum John	23	"	"
Gifford Frank	18	"	"
Hanson Parker W.	18	"	"
Hartwell Joseph W.	23	"	"
Haskell Charles F.	19	"	"
Jewell Charles C.	18	"	"
Libby John F.	44	"	"
Locke Cyrus	24	"	"
Mansfield John R.	41	"	"
McMurphy Benjamin F.	35	"	"
McMahon Philip	27	"	"
McNeil Michael	28	"	"
Melcher Levi L.	27	"	"
Miner Albert H.	36	"	"
Murphy William H.	18	"	"
Parsons Cyrus	42	"	"
Parshley Sylvester	18	"	Disability—Sept 26, '62.
Phillips Phineas W.	26	"	Expiration of service, Dec. 31, '62
Rice Benjamin B.	34	"	"
Shatswell Joseph A.	27	"	"
Shaw Neil	25	"	"
Smith Harley P.	45	"	"

NAMES AND RANK.	AGE.	DATE OF MUSTER.	TERMINATION OF SERVICE, &C.
Smith William R.	38	July 1, '64	Expiration of service, Dec. 31, 1862.
Soley Franklin	18	"	" " "
Southwick Elbridge M.	18	"	" " "
Symonds Stephen G.	30	"	" " "
Upham Benjamin N.	26	"	" " "
Walton John H.	21	"	" " "
Welch Michael	22	"	" " "
West George	30	"	" " "
Whitmore William W.	40	Oct. 22, '62	" " "
Wiley Edwin W.	18	July 1, '62	" " "

Fifth Regiment Infantry, M.V.M.,—Nine Months.

NAMES AND RANK.	AGE.	DATE OF MUSTER.	TERMINATION OF SERVICE, &C.
George H. Peirson, Col.	46	Oct. 8, '62	Expiration of service, July 2, 1863.
John M. Foster, Hosp. Steward.	36	"	" " "

Company C.

PRIVATES.	AGE.	DATE OF MUSTER.	TERMINATION OF SERVICE, &C.
Foster John M.	36	Sept. 16, '62	Hosp. Stew'd, Oct. 8, '62
Hadley Horace L.	25	"	Expiration of service, July 2, 1863.
Harrington William H.	18	"	" " "
Johnson Frank E.	18	"	" " "
Low George H.	20	"	" " "
Lunt William J.	33	"	" " "

Forty-Eighth Regiment Infantry M V.M.,—Nine Months

NAMES AND RANK.	AGE.	DATE OF MUSTER.	TERMINATION OF SERVICE, &C.
George Wheatland, Major.	23	Dec. 8, '62	Expiration of service, Sept. 3, '63.
Horace W. Durgin, Qr. Mr.	23	"	" " "
John G. Robinson, Qr. Mr. Sergt	22	"	" " "

Company A.

PRIVATE.	AGE.	DATE OF MUSTER.	TERMINATION OF SERVICE, &C.
Stover Nathaniel F.	34	Sept. 16, '62	Expiration of service, Sept. 3, '63.

PATRIOTS OF SALEM.

Company E.

NAMES AND RANK.	AGE.	DATE OF MUSTER.	TERMINATION OF SERVICE, &c.
George Wheatland, jr. Capt.	23	Sept. 19, '62	Major, Dec. 8, '62.
Charles Saunders, 1st Lieut.	20	Dec. 12, '62	Resigned June 20, '63.
John F. Ford, " "	25	July 24, '63	Expiration of service, Sept. 3, '63.
Charles Saunders, 2nd Lieut.	20	Sept. 19, '62	1st Lieut. Dec. 12, '63.
Charles J. Lee " "	23	Dec. 12, '62	Resigned March 10, '63.
John F. Ford " "	25	May 9, '63	1st Lieut. July 24, '63.
George Wiley " "	23	July 24, '63	Expiration of service, Sept. 3, '63.
Samuel W. Larrabee, 1st Sergt.	24	Sept. 19, '62	" "
Charles C. Hoyt, Sergt.	23	"	" "
Thomas E. Jewett "	26	"	" "
Charles J. Lee "	23	"	2d Lieut. Dec. 12, '62.
John F. Ford "	25	"	2d Lieut. May 9, '62.
Wm. Daniels, Corp.	38	"	Expiration of service, Sept. 3, '63.
Joseph N. Larrabee, Corp.	33	"	" "
Charles A. Brown "	21	"	" "
James Walsh "	24	"	" "
James F. Nelson "	25	"	" "
PRIVATES.			
Bousley Theophilus S.	18	"	Killed June 12, '63, at Port Hudson.
Brown Thomas W.	37	"	Expiration of service, Sept. 3, '63.
Callahan John	20	Nov. 14, '62	" "
Chase John R.	18	Sept. 19, '62	" "
Coggin Thomas	18	"	" "
Colwell Patrick	25	"	" "
Cross George	19	"	" "
Daniels Edward A.	27	"	" "
Daniels John B.	32	"	" "
Dockham William S.	40	"	" "
Douglass Albert	18	"	Transferred March 7, '63, 2d R.I. Cav.
Farley George E.	18	"	Expiration of service, Sept. 3, '63.
Flakefield John jr.	35	"	" "
Foote George F.	21	"	Disability—January 1, '63.
Ford Jeremiah L.	28	"	Expiration of service, Sept. 3, '63.
Francis Joseph	40	"	" "
Gray George A.	29	"	" "
Griffin Thomas J.	36	"	" "
Hanson George	26	"	Deserted Oct. 1, '62, Wenham, Mass.
Hazelton Andrew	42	"	Disability—May 11, '63.
Hinds Richard	22	"	Expiration of service, Sept. 3, '63.
Ingalls John D.	35	"	" "
Jackson Andrew	21	Sept. 21, '62	Deserted Nov. 28, '62, Wenham, Mass.
Jaques Joseph	21	Sept. 19, '62	" Sept. 25, '62, " "
Jeffreys William F.	21	"	Expiration of service, Sept. 3, '63.
Kennedy Michael	18	"	Transferred March 7, '63, 2d R. I. Cav.
Larrabee Warren	33	"	Expiration of service, Sept. 3, '63.
Lyons James	21	Nov. 14, '62	Deserted Nov. 14, '62, Wenham, Mass.
Lynch Patrick	27	" 17, '62	Expiration of service, Sept. 3, '63.
Mathews Vincent	40	Sept. 19, '62	" "
McCabe Patrick	37	"	" "
Mitchell Patrick	30	"	" "
Morton Charles	22	Nov. 14, '62	Deserted Nov. 14, '62, Readville, Mass.
Murphy John	40	Sept. 19, '62	Expiration of service, Sept. 3, '63.
Murphy Michael	44	"	" "
Murphy Peter	18	"	" "
Powers Stephen A.	33	Oct. 13, '62	" "

PATRIOTS OF SALEM.

NAMES AND RANK.	AGE.	DATE OF MUSTER.	TERMINATION OF SERVICE, &c.
Ronan William H.	26	Sept. 19, '62	Expiration of service, Sept. 3, '63.
Scully Patrick	20	"	" "
Shaw Walter G. C. C.	20	"	" "
Smith Patrick	35	"	Died at Salem, Sept. 10, '63.
Southwick Edward	29	"	Expiration of service, Sept. 3, '63.
Stacey Peter	33	"	" "
Stimpson Edward A.	26	"	Transferred to 16th Mass. Reg.
Sweeney William	41	"	Expiration of service, Sept. 3, '63.
Symonds Joseph P.	18	Nov. 19, '62	" "
Very Ephraim P.	35	Sept. 19, '62	" "
Veno Felix	24	"	" "
Walton Joseph A.	40	"	" "
Williams Martin V.	28	"	" "
Wiley George	23	"	2d Lieut. July 24, '63.
Wiley Moses jr.	27	"	Expiration of service, Sept. 3, '63.
Wiley Mark L.	18	"	Disability,—Dec. 24, '62.
Wippich John	34	"	Expiration of service, Sept. 3, '63.

Company F.

NAMES AND RANK.	AGE.	DATE OF MUSTER.	TERMINATION OF SERVICE, &c.
Servington S. Burnett, 2d Lieut.	35	June 24, '63	Expiration of service, Sept. 3, '63.
Servington S. Burnett, Corp.	35	Nov. 6, '62	2d Lieut. June 24, '63.
Thomas F. Hines "	18	Nov. 3, '62	Expiration of service, Sept. 23, '63.
William H. Walsh, Musician.	18	"	" "
PRIVATES.			
Bateman Joseph	28	"	" "
Bateman Thomas	44	"	" "
Chase George E.	18	"	" "
Flood John	18	"	" "
Hazelton Augustus	34	"	" "
Hovey William	35	"	" "
Marshall William F.	23	Nov. 11, '62	" "
McDugal John	30	Nov. 7, '62	" "
Ryan Patrick	33	Nov. 3, '62	Deserted Nov. 14, '62, Wenham, Mass.
Tucker John H.	40	"	Expiration of service, Sept. 3, '63.

Fiftieth Regiment Infantry, M.V.M.—Nine Months.

NAMES AND RANK.	AGE.	DATE OF MUSTER.	TERMINATION OF SERVICE, &c.
John Hodges jr., Major	21	Nov. 11, '62	Expiration of service, Aug. 24, '63.

Company A.

NAMES AND RANK.	AGE.	DATE OF MUSTER.	TERMINATION OF SERVICE, &c.
George D. Putman, Capt.	27	Sept. 15, '62	Expiration of service, Aug. 24, '63.
Robert W. Reeves, 1st Lieut.	21	"	" "

NAMES AND RANK.	AGE.	DATE OF MUSTER.	TERMINATION OF SERVICE, &C.
Wm. B. Upton, 2nd Lieut.	24	Sept. 15, '62	Expiration of service, Aug 24, '63.
Nathan A. Frye, 1st Sergt.	22	"	" "
Geo. O. Stevens, Sergt.	25	"	" "
John W. Evans "	20	"	" "
David E. Saunders, jr., Sergt.	20	"	" "
Augustus Brown "	19	"	" "
Gilman A. Andrews, Corp.	21	"	" "
George H. Blinn "	21	"	" "
William D. Balch - "	26	"	" "
William H. Dalrymple "	20	"	" "
Jeremiah Nelson - "	26	"	" "
Nathaniel F. Robinson "	18	"	" "
Greanleaf S. Tukey "	19	"	" "
John F. Simon - "	19	"	Died April 18, '63, Baton Rouge, La.
Edmund Stillman, Musician	15	Oct. 28, '62	Expiration of service, Aug. 24, '63.
Elias A. Trofatter, Wagoner	24	Sept. 15, '62	Died July 30, '63, enroute home.
PRIVATES.			
Allen Charles F. -	19	"	Expiration of service, Aug 24, '63
Babbidge William A.	20	"	" "
Baker Henry C. -	25	"	Deserted Dec. 10, '62, at N. Y. City.
Barker Charles F.	21	Nov. 1, '62	Expiration of service, Aug. 24, '63
Barenson Abram F.	20	Oct. 31, '62	" "
Bennett George A.	18	Sept. 15, '62	" "
Boden Thomas C.	44	Oct. 6, '62	" "
Bousley Nathaniel C.	19	Sept. 15, '62	" "
Bovey Thomas L.	19	Oct. 6, '62	" "
Brooks Horace A.	18	Sept. 15, '62	" "
Brown William P.	19	"	" "
Bryant Timothy W.	21	"	" "
Chessman Charles H.	41	"	" "
Clark William B. -	24	"	Deserted Dec. 10, '62, N.Y.
Copeland George A.	18	Oct. 31, '62	Expiration of service, Aug. 24, '63
Cook George B. -	18	Sept. 15, '62	" "
Dalrymple George	18	"	" "
Dodge Joseph R. -	18	"	Died, July 26, '63, Port Hudson, La.
Eaton Horace D. -	18	"	Expiration of service, Aug. 24, '63.
Evans William	26	Oct. 31, '62	" "
Finley Edward	18	Sept. 15, '62	Died, Feb. 23, '63, Baton Rouge, La.
Friend Joel M. -	19	"	Expiration of service, Aug. 24, '63.
Gardner Charles W.	23	"	" "
Gardner William H.	20	"	" "
Glover Joseph N. -	22	"	" "
Glover William H.	23	"	" "
Hale Joseph S. -	19	"	" "
Hall William H. -	19	"	" "
Hammond William G.	20	"	" "
Harris Alphonzo -	20	"	" "
Harris William S.	21	"	" "
Harrington Leonard	21	"	" "
Janes John	21	"	" "
Kendall William H.	20	"	" "
Knowlton George -	21	"	Died, April 7, '63, Baton Rouge, La.
Lamson George A.	18	"	Expiration of service, Aug. 24, '63.
Langdell George W.	19	"	" "
Lee Joseph	28	"	" "
Lowd Jacob R. -	21	"	" "
Luscomb George W.	28	"	" "
Mackie John A. -	18	"	" "
Morse George F. -	20	"	" "
Newton Albert E. -	24	"	" "

NAMES AND RANK.	AGE.	DATE OF MUSTER.	TERMINATION OF SERVICE, &c.
Nichols George A.	18	Sept. 15, '62	Expiration of service, Aug. 24, '63.
Noble James A.	18	"	" "
Ober Oliver	20	"	" "
Palmer William H. H.	22	"	" "
Perchard Clement H.	20	"	" "
Perkins Charles	19	"	" "
Perkins Francis M.	18	"	" "
Perkins George H.	20	"	" "
Perkins James W.	19	"	" "
Perley Thomas A.	18	"	" "
Peterson Andrew G.	19	"	" "
Pickman Hersey D.	19	"	" "
Pond Frederick A.	21	"	" "
Pope Thomas S.	34	"	" "
Preston Otis P.	19	Oct. 31, '62	Died, May 26, '63, Baton Rouge, La.
Preston William A.	19	Sept. 15, '62	Expiration of service, Aug. 24, '63.
Robinson John	19	"	" "
Safford George W.	18	"	" "
Sanborn Joseph W.	19	Oct. 6, '62	" "
Scriggins William J.	28	Sept. 15, '62	" "
Short Charles H.	19	"	" "
Skinner James N.	23	"	" "
Sleuman Charles A.	19	"	" "
Southard George F.	21	"	Disability—March 3, '63.
Stillman Amos	19	Oct. 13, '62	Expiration of service, Aug. 24, '63.
Stoddard George A.	18	Sept. 15, '62	" "
Stratton Benjamin F.	27	"	Died, May 1, '63, Baton Rouge, La.
Symonds Edward A.	20	"	Expiration of service, Aug. 24, '63.
Thorndike Theodore A.	18	"	" "
Trask James E.	20	"	" "
Tuttle William W.	19	"	" "
Upton Warren A.	31	"	" "
Warner Frank B.	18	"	" "
Waters James V.	23	"	Died Aug. 1, '63, enroute home.
Woodbury George H.	20	"	Expiration of service, Aug. 24, '63.

Company B.

John L. Ward, Capt.	20	Sept. 15, '62.	Resigned July 24, '63.
Edward W. Phillips, 1st Lieut.	20	"	" " 13, '63.
William H. Hurd 2nd Lieut.	31	"	Expiration of service, Aug. 24, '63.
PRIVATES.			
Foss John G.	22	"	" "
Miller James	19	"	" "

Company D.

Cook George W.	28	Sept. 19, '62.	Expiration of service, Aug. 24, '63.

PATRIOTS OF SALEM.

Fourth Battery Light Artillery,—Three Years.

NAMES AND RANK.	AGE.	DATE OF MUSTER.	TERMINATION OF SERVICE, &C.
Charles Manning, Capt.	40	Nov. 27, '61	Resigned Oct. 20, '62.
Henry Davidson, 1st Lieut.	43	Aug. 17, '62	Resigned as 2d Lieut. Jan. 31, '62.
Joseph B. Briggs " "	30	July 19, '63	Expiration of service, Oct. 12, 65.
Thomas H. Manning, 1st Lieut.	27	Oct. 13, 65	Expiration as 2d Lieut., Oct. 12, '65.
Henry Davidson, 2nd Lieut.	43	Nov. 27, '61	1st Lieut. Aug. 17, '62.
Joseph B. Briggs " "	28	Aug. 17, '62	" July 19, '63.
Thomas H. Manning, 2nd Lieut.	25	Aug. 15, '63	" Oct. 13, '65.
John Hurley, Q. M. S.	21	Jan. 3, '61	Expiration of service, Nov. 10, '65.
Benjamin W. Lander, Q. M. S.	39	Oct. 9, '61	Disability—Oct. 5, '62.
Joseph B. Briggs, 1st Sergt.	28	Sept. 5, '61	2d Lieut. Aug. 17, '62.
Henry T. Manning	23	" 6, "	" " 15, '63.
Nicholas Bovey, Sergt.	43	Nov. 8, '61	Disability—Aug. 22, '63.
Charles A. D. Clark, Sergt.	20	Sept. 5, '61	Re-enlisted Jan. 2, '64.
Thomas Mulready "	20	Dec. 26, '63	Expiration of service, Oct. 14, '65.
Charles B. Newcomb jr. "	24	Sept. 17, '61	Re-enlisted Jan. 4, '64.
Charles B. Newcomb jr. "	26	Jan. 5, '64	Expiration of service, Oct. 14, '65.
Franklin B. Smith "	27	Jan. 3, 64	" "
Benjamin F. Vanderford "	37	" 5, "	" " Nov. 10, '65.
Samuel P. Williston "	32	Sept. 13, '61	Disability—Oct. 17, '62.
Henry M. Clark Corp.	21	Jan. 3, '64	Expiration of service, Nov. 10, '65.
Moses H. Littlefield "	40	Sept. 6, '61	Disability—June 9, '62.
Edwin F. Pratt "	20	" 5, "	Re-enlisted Jan. 2, '64.
Edwin F. Pratt "	22	Jan. 3, '64	Expiration of service, Oct. 14, '65.
Franklin B. Smith "	25	Sept. 23, '61	Re-enlisted Jan. 2, '64.
Benjamin F. Vanderford, Corp.	35	Dec. 17, '61	" " 4, "
Epes Cogswell, Artificer	41	Nov. 2, '61	Died at Fort Pike, La., Nov. 12, '62.
Moses D. Faunce "	40	Sept. 9, '61	Re-enlisted Jan. 3, '64.
Moses D. Faunce "	42	Jan. 4, '64	Expiration of service, Oct. 14, '65.
Daniel A. Manning "	30	Nov. 16, '61	Died at New Orleans, La. Oct. 28, '62.
PRIVATES.			
Barnard Samuel	45	Sept. 30, '61	Died at Fort Pike, La., Nov. 13, '62.
Boyce John F.	21	Nov. 3, '61	" " " 3, "
Briggs Edward L. P.	18	Nov. 2, '61	Disability—May 18, '62.
Brown Jeremiah W.	19	Feb. 24, '64	Expiration of service, Oct. 14, '65.
Burns John H.	28	Sept. 9, '61	Disability—March 27, '63.
Chapman Lewis A.	18	" 1, '64	Transferred Jan. 17, '65, to 13th Bat.
Clark Charles A. D.	18	Nov. 18, '61	Re-enlisted Jan. 2, '64.
Clark Henry M.	19	" "	" "
Collins John H.	39	" 6, '61	" Dec. 25, '63.
Collins John H.	41	Dec. 26, '63	Expiration of service, Oct. 14, '65.
Cotter Simon	34	Nov. 13, '61	Re-enlisted Dec. 25, '63.
Cotter Simon	36	Dec. 26, '63	Expiration of service, Nov. 10, '65.
Cowee George L.	34	Nov. 8, '61	Died at New Orleans, Oct. 23, '63.
Curtis Jacob	25	Oct. 28, '61	Re-enlisted Dec. 25, '63.
Daley John	18	Feb 29, '64	Rejected Recruit, March 3, '64.
Davidson Henry jr.	20	Oct. 28, '61	Re-enlisted Dec. 25, '63.
Davidson Henry jr.	22	" 26, '63	Expiration of service, Oct. 14, '65.
Davis James B.	39	Sept. 12, '61	Died at New Orleans, La. Sept. 24, '62.
Derwin Michael	26	Aug. 31, '64	Expiration of service, Aug. 31, '65.
Donahue Thomas	36	Oct. 19, '61	Died at N. O. La., Nov. 13, '62.
Duffee John R.	34	Sept. 16, '61	Re-enlisted Jan. 2, '64.
Duffee John R.	36	Jan. 3, '64	Expiration of service, Oct. 14, '65.
Dwinell William P.	19	Sept. 30, '64	Transferred Jan. 17, '65, to 13th Bat.
Edwards John L.	26	" 17, '61	Re-enlisted Jan. 3, '64.
Foote Moses F.	24	Nov. 1, '61	Died at N. O. La., Oct. 28, '62.

NAMES AND RANK.	AGE.	DATE OF MUSTER.	TERMINATION OF SERVICE, &c.
Garrity Patrick	26	Oct. 25, '64	Transferred Jan. 17, '65 to 13th Bat.
Gilman Joseph	39	Sept. 9, '61	" June 11, '64 to V. R. Corps.
Goodhue John E.	22	"	Re-enlisted Jan. 2, '64.
Goodhue John E.	24	Jan. 3, '64	Expiration of service, Oct. 14, '65.
Griffin William	20	Sept. 30, '61	Re-enlisted Dec. 25, '63.
Griffin William	22	Dec. 26, '63	Expiration of service, Oct. 14, '65.
Grover John jr.	35	Sept. 19, '61	Re-enlisted Dec. 25, '63.
Grover John jr.	37	Dec. 26, '63	Expiration of service, Oct. 14, '65.
Hart Joseph L.	36	Oct. 19, '61	Died at Fort Pike, La., Dec. 1, '62.
Hayford William	40	Sept. 21, '61	Disability July 5, '62.
Hazelton David jr.	25	Nov. 18, '61	Re-enlisted Jan. 2, '64.
Hazelton David jr.	27	Jan. 3, '64	Expiration of service, Oct. 10, '65.
Hennessey James P.	19	Feb. 24, '64	" " " 4, "
Huntress John E.	22	Sept. 13, '61	Re-enlisted Dec. 25, '63.
Huntress John E.	24	Dec. 26, '63	Expiration of service, Oct. 14, '65.
Hurley John	19	Sept. 28, '61	Re-enlisted Jan. 2, '64.
Huse Stephen S.	18	Nov. 18, '61	" Dec. 25, '63.
Henry Johnson	22	Jan. 3, '64	Expiration of service, Nov. 10, '65.
Kezar Albert	44	Oct. 1, '61	Disability—Oct. 21, '62.
Kilbride Daniel	34	Nov. 12, '61	" Aug. 24, '63.
Kingsley George W.	21	Sept. 13, '61	" Oct. 17, '62.
Looby Thomas	20	" 6, '61	Re-enlisted Jan. 2, '64.
Looby Thomas	22	Jan. 3, '64	Expiration of service, Oct. 14, '64.
Maddin John	21	Aug. 31, '64	Transferred Jan. 17, '65, to 13th Bat.
Mayner John	32	Nov. 13, '61	Re-enlisted Dec. 25, '63.
Mayner John	34	Dec. 26, '63	Died at Galveston, Texas, July 30, '65
Marshall John H.	23	Sept. 24, '64	Transferred Jan. 17, '65, to 13th Bat.
Marr Michael	18	Feb. 24, '64	Rejected Recruit, March 3, '64.
McCarty John	25	Oct. 22, '61	Re-enlisted Jan. 2, '64.
McCarty John	27	Jan. 3, '64	Drowned, Miss. River, Sept. 6, '64.
Melley William J.	18	Oct. 25, '61	Died at N. O. La., Feb. 11, '63.
Munroe George	45	Oct. 31, '61	" " Aug 31, '62.
Morgan Michael	18	Feb. 24, '64	Expiration of service, Oct. 14, '65.
Mulready Thomas	18	Sept. 18, '61	Re-enlisted Dec. 25, '63.
Nolan Thomas	21	Feb. 25, '64	Transferred to 13th Battery.
Parsons Eben O.	20	Sept. 5, '61	Re-enlisted Jan. 2, '64.
Parsons Eben O.	22	Jan. 4, '64	Expiration of service, Oct. 14, '65.
Peabody William M.	19	Sept. 12, '61	Re-enlisted Jan. 2, '64.
Peabody William M.	21	Jan. 3, '64	Expiration of service, Oct 14, '65.
Phippen David	23	Nov. 18, '61	Disability, Oct. 17, '62.
Pratt Calvin L.	21	Sept. 13, '61	Re-enlisted Jan. 2, '64.
Pratt Calvin L.	23	Jan. 3, '64	Expiration of service, Oct. 14, '65.
Ramsdell Alonzo O.	20	Sept. 28, 64	Transferred Jan. 17, '65 to 13th Bat.
Rust Edwin F.	21	" 3, '64	" " " " "
Sheehan John J.	19	Feb. 24, 64	Expiration of service, Oct. 14, '65.
Silver Augustus	39	Sept. 19, '61	Re-enlisted Jan. 2, '64.
Silver Augustus	41	Jan. 3, 64	Expiration of service, Oct. 14, '65.
Silver William A.	18	Aug. 26, '64	Transferred to 13th Battery.
Skerry George L.	26	Sept. 8, '61	Disability Sept. 21, '64.
Thompson Franklin B.	25	Nov. 1, 61	Died July 27, '62 at Carrollton, La.
Thrasher Nathaniel	32	" 13, '61	Re-enlisted Jan. 4, '64.
Thrasher Nathaniel	34	Jan. 5, '64	Died, at Memphis Tenn., April 8, '65.
Trask Henry A.	23	Sept. 9, '61	Transferred May 1, '64, V. R. Corps.
Trull Charles W.	23	" 22, "	Died at Fort Pike, Nov. 11, '62.
Tucker William W.	19	March 8, '64	Expiration of service, Oct. 13, '65
Warner Edward L.	32	Sept. 10, '61	Re-enlisted Jan. 3, 64.
Warner Edward L.	34	Jan. 4, '64	Expiration of service, Oct. 14, '65.
Warner John V.	33	Sept. 5, '61	Re-enlisted Sept. 27, '64.
Warner John V.	35	Feb. 28, '64	Transferred Jan. 17, '65, to 13th Bat.
Welch Michael	28	Nov. 4, '61	Re-enlisted April 20, '64.
Welch Michael	30	April, 21, 64	Died Cairo, Ill. Jan. 16, '65.

PATRIOTS OF SALEM. 25

NAMES AND RANK.	AGE.	DATE OF MUSTER.	TERMINATION OF SERVICE, &C.
Wentworth John H.	28	Dec. 17, '61	Died N. O. La., May 26, '62.
Weston Charles	25	Feb. 6, '64	Expiration of service Oct. 14, '65.
Whiarty Thomas	18	Sept. 13, '61	*Re-enlisted Dec. 25, '63.
" "	20	Dec. 26, '63	Expiration of service Oct. 14, '65.
Wildes Hayward	18	Sept. 6, '64	Transferred Jan. 17, '65, to 13th Bat.
Williams William D.	23	Sept. 17, '61	Disability March 26, '63.

Fifth Battery Light Artillery,—Three Years.

NAMES AND RANK.	AGE.	DATE OF MUSTER.	TERMINATION OF SERVICE, &C.
Charles A. Phillips, Capt.	24	Oct. 18, '62	Expiration of service, Brevet Major, June 12, '65.
" " " 1st Lieut.	21	July 13, '62	Capt., Oct. 18, '62.
Samuel H. Hamblett "	22	Oct. 14, '64	Expiration of service June 12, '65.
Charles A. Phillips, 2nd Lieut.	20	Oct. 8, '61	1st Lieut. July 13, '62.
Samuel H. Hamblett " "	20	June 19, '64	" Oct. 4, '64.
PRIVATES.			
Balfe Thomas	21	Aug. 9, '64	
Buckley John	21	Aug 24, '64	Expiration of service, June 12, '65.
Griffin Thomas	39	Dec. 9, '62	Re-enlisted Feb. 6, '64.
" "	41	Feb. 9, '64	Expiration of service, June 12, '65.
Murphy John	38	Dec. 9 '62	Disability, April 12, '64.
" "	44	Aug. 22, '64	Expiration of service, June 12, '65.
Murphy Thomas	27	Aug. 5, '64	" "
OBrien John	43	Dec. 10, '62	Disability Dec. 28, '63.
OHara Patrick	43	Dec. 10, '62	Disability Sept. 15, '63.
Purbeck William L.	18	Dec 13, '62	Killed at Gettysburg, Pa., July 2, '63.
Roberts William	21	Oct. 21, '64	Expiration of service, June 12, '65.

Thirteenth Battery Light Artillery,—Three Years.

NAMES AND RANK.	AGE.	DATE OF MUSTER.	TERMINATION OF SERVICE, &C.
Chapman Lewis A.	18	Sept. 1, '64	Expiration of service, June, 16, '65.
Dwinnell William P.	19	Sept. 30, '64	" "
Garrity Patrick	26	Oct. 25, '64	Expiration of service, July 28, '65.
Lynch Patrick	31	Oct. 13, '64	" "
Marshall John H.	23	Sept. 24, '64	Expiration of service June 16, '65.
Nolan Thomas	21	Feb. 26, '64	Died Jan. 8, '65, Memphis, Tenn.
Ramsdell Alonzo O.	21	Sept. 18, '64	Expiration of service, June 16, '65.
Rust Edwin F.	21	Sept. 3, '64	Expiration of service May 25, '65.
Silver William A.	18	Aug. 26, '64	Expiration of service, June 16, '65.
Warner John V.	35	Feb. 28 '64	Expiration of service July 28, '65.

4

First Regiment Heavy Artillery,—Three Years.

NAMES AND RANK.	AGE.	DATE OF MUSTER.	TERMINATION OF SERVICE, &C.
Thomas R. Tannatt, Col.	30	Nov. 8, '62	Resigned July 18, '64.
Samuel C. Oliver Lieut. Col	31	July 5, '61	Resigned March 13, '62, Brevet Col.
Seth G. Buxton, Major.	29	June 10, '62	Died Jan. 15, '63.
Seth S. Buxton, Capt.	28	July 5, '61	Major, June 10, '62.
James Pope Capt.	24	June 10, '62	Expiration of service, Oct. 28, '64.
Frank Pope "	24	March 27, '65	Expiration of service, March 27, '65.
John C. Chadwick, 1st Lieut.	39	July 6, '61	not mustered, Adj't, 19 Inf., Aug. 22, '61.
James Pope, "	22	"	Capt. June. 10, '62.
Edward Hobbs, "	23	June 10, '62	Disability June 18, '64.
Samuel Dalton, "	30	June 7, '62	Expiration of service, Oct. 7, '64.
Joseph C. Smith, "	32	March 19, '62	Resigned Sept. 14, '63.
Benjamin C. Harrod, 1st Lieut.	34	Oct. 25, 62	Resigned Feb. 24, '63.
Frank Pope, "	22	March 19, '62	Expiration of service, Oct. 7, '64 Capt. March 27, '65.
Edward Hobbs, 2nd Lieut.	23	Jan. 18, '62	1st Lieut. Jan. 10, '62.
Benjamin C. Harrod, 2nd Lieut.	33	March 19, '62	" Jan. 16, '62.
Frank Pope, 2nd Lieut.	22	Feb. 15, '62	" March 19, '63.
Samuel Dalton, 2nd Lieut.	30	"	" June 7, '62.
James W. Goss, "	27	Aug. 2, '63	" April 9, '65.
Henfield Amos, Sergt. Major.	40	July 5, '61	Promotion Oct. 4, '62.
Webb J. F., Com.	23	"	Expiration of service, July 8, '65.

Company A.

	AGE.	DATE OF MUSTER.	TERMINATION OF SERVICE, &C.
Phelan Thomas J., Corp.	19	July 31. '62	Expiration of service, July 8, '64.
Walden William W. P., Corp.	25	Aug. 6, '62	" "
PRIVATES.			
Arnold James E.	25	Jan. 23, '63	Transferred to V. R. Corps Jan. 2, ,65.
Bickford Jefferson A.	25	Aug. 6, '62	Expiration of service July 8, '64.
Brown Samuel	41	"	" "
Dougherty Michael S.	28	"	Transferred to V. R. Cops Jan. 11 '64.
Farmer Joseph P.	30	June 22, '63	Disability July 31, '65.
Gammon James	21	July 5, '61	Re-enlisted Nov. 27, '63.
Gammon James	23	Nov. 28, '63	Missing in action Oct. 2, '64.
Heeney William A.	27	Aug. 5, '62	Expiration of service, July 8, '64.
Hersey William H.	30	Aug. 6, '62	" "
Hopkins John	30	"	" "
Horton George	32	"	" "
Lusk Joseph H.	27	"	" "
Morse John	42	"	Disability, May 4, '64.
Orsborne Laban S.	21	"	To Re-enlist Dec. 30, 63.
Orsborne Laban S.	23	Dec. 31, '63	Expiration of service, June 7, '64.
Phillips John	43	Aug. 6, '62	To Re-enlist Dec. 30 '63.
Phippen Charles H.	23	June 22, '63	Expiration of service, June 19, '65.
Phippen Robert A.	29	Aug. 5, '62	Expiration of service July 8, '64.
Phippen Robert C.	23	Aug. 6, '62	" "
Phippen William H.	29	"	" "
Pitman William	34	"	" "
Ross William P.	19	Feb. 27 '62	Expiration of service Jan. 22, '65.
Smith Thomas R	24	Aug. 8, '62	Expiration of service, July 8, '64.

PATRIOTS OF SALEM.   27

NAMES AND RANK.	AGE.	DATE OF MUSTER.	TERMINATION OF SERVICE, &C.
Trainer Thomas	20	July 5, '61	Expiration of service, July 8, '64.
Tucker Joseph W.	33	Aug. 2, '62	" "
Upham Franklin	29	Aug. 5, '62	" "
Upham Warren Joseph	23	Aug. 6, '62	" "
Wiggin Benjamin F.	30	"	" "
Wood William P.	43	Aug. 4, '62	Transferred to Co. F. 18th V. R. Corps, July '63.

Company C.

	AGE.	DATE OF MUSTER.	TERMINATION OF SERVICE, &C.
Atherton Charles H., 1st Sergt.	27	Dec. 21, '63	2nd Lieut July 9, '64.
Andrews Richard F., "	28	Jan. 5, '64	2nd Lieut. Nov. 12, '64 U. S. C. T.
Henderson Ephraim I., "	19	Aug. 6, '62	Expiration of service, July 8 '64.
Pool Marcus M., Sergt.	23	Dec. 22, '63	2nd Lieut. Oct. 6, '64.
Bruce Robert P. Corp.	33	Aug. 15, 62	Expiration of service, July 8, '64.
Henderson Charles H , Corp.	22	Aug. 6, '62	" "
Phipps Henry B , Corp.	25	Aug. 15, '62	Died at Andersonville, Ga. Aug. 26, '64
Snell Nicholas P., "	18	Aug. 6, '62	Died of wounds Wash'n June 11, '64

PRIVATES.

	AGE.	DATE OF MUSTER.	TERMINATION OF SERVICE, &C.
Batchelder Charles	20	Feb. 29, '64	Expiration of service, in Co. M. Aug. 16, '65.
Patchelder Charles	18	July 15, '62	To Re-enlist Feb. 28, '64.
Bickford John M.	32	Aug. 6, '62	Expiration of service, (absent sick) July 8, '64.
Bowler Henry A.	18	Aug. 4, '64	Died at Andersonville, Ga. Sept 1, '64.
Carroll Peter	23	Aug. 16, '62	Expiration of service, July 8, '64.
Chipman James G.	35	Aug. 6, '62	" " (absent sick) July 8, '64.
Fairfield Samuel G.	42	July 28, '62	" "
Fairfield William	33	"	Expiration of service, July 8, '64.
Flowers William H. jr.	18	Aug. 6, '62	" "
Foster Charles W	21	Oct. 27, '63	Expiration of service, Co M, Aug. 16, '65
Foster Patrick	38	Aug. 2, '62	Died at Fort Tillinghast Feb. 9, '64.
Gardner Howard P.	18	Aug. 1, '62	Expiration of service, May 17, '65.
Gillespie James S	21	Aug. 6, '61	Disability March 27, '63.
Gorman James	33	July 22, '62	Disability Aug. 30, '63.
Hathaway Stephen F.	27	Aug. 6, '62	To Re-enlist Jan. 31, '64.
Herrick Benjamin jr.	36	July 31, '62	" Jan 4, '64.
Howard Eben M	20	Aug 6, '62	Expiration of service, July 8, '64.
Neal James M	22	"	Disability March 19, '63.
Parrott Francis	30	"	Expiration of service, (absent sick) July 8, '64.
Perry Horace S.	19	"	Expiration of service, (absent sick) July 8, '64.
Poor James jr.	31	"	Expiration of service, July 8, '64.
Pratt James F.	19	July 25, '61	" "
Ross Joseph H.	26	July 23, '62	" "
Tarbox Jonathan S.	21	Dec. 22, '63	Expiration of service, July 20, '65.
Varney Henry	22	Aug. 6, '62	" " " 8, '64.
Watts Charles jr.	18	July 28, '62	" "

PATRIOTS OF SALEM.

Company D.

NAMES AND RANK.	AGE.	DATE OF MUSTER.	TERMINATION OF SERVICE, &c.
Cutler Nathan F., 1st Sergt.	19	July 5, '61	Expiration of service July 8, '64.
Hobbs Edward "	22	"	2nd Lieut. Jan. 18, '65.
Dalton Samuel, Sergt.	21	"	1st Lieut. June 7, '62.
Dalton Sepherino M., Sergt.	28	Dec. 31, '63	Supernumerary, July 31, '65.
Dwinell David L. M., "	35	July 5, '61	Expiration of service, July 8, '64.
Millett Andrew J., "	27	"	" "
Pope Frank, "	20	"	2nd Lieut., Feb. 15, '62.
Williams John H ,	20	Feb. 16, '64	Expiration of service, Co. I, Aug. 16, '65
Beckett Daniel C., Corp.	18	July 5, '61	Expiration of service, July 8, '64.
Lewis Chancy H., "	29	"	Disability March 7, '63.
Maxfield Charles O., Corp.	28	Dec. 8, '63	Supernumerary July 31, '65.
Shaw John, Corp.	26	Feb. 20, '64	Expiration of service, Co. I, Aug. 16, '65
Swasey Lewis G., Corp.	19	July 5, '61	Disability Feb. 16, '63.
Warner Clarence A., Corp.	19	"	Expiration of service, July 8. '64.
Hobbs George, Artificer	42	Dec. 18, '63	Disability, June 14, '65.

PRIVATES.

Adams Charles	41	July 5, '61	To Re-enlist Dec. 17, '63.
Adams Charles	43	Dec. 18, '63	Expiration of service, Aug, 16, '65, Co I
Arnold Joseph E.	34	Aug. 1, '62	To Re-enlist Dec. 28, '63.
Arnold Joseph E.	36	Dec. 29, '63	Expiration of service, Aug. 16, '65, Co. I
Begg William H.	23	July 5, '61	Expiration of service, July 8, '64.
Buxton Augustus	28	"	" "
Clark John F.	29	Aug. 5, '62	Expiration of service, July 8, '64
Collier Charles D.	26	July 5, '61	" "
Cook Adelbert P.	18	July 5, '61	" "
Cowley John H.	26	Aug. 4, '62	Transferred Jan. 11, '64, to V.R. Corps.
Dalton Eleazer M. J.	36	Dec. 30, '61	To re-enlist, Dec. 30, '63.
Dalton Eleazer M. J.	38	Dec. 31, '63	Killed June 22, '64, Petersburg, Va.
Dalton Sepherino M.	26	July 5, '61	To re-enlist, Dec. 30, '63.
Davis Andrew L.	18	July 5, '61	Deserted, Feb. 26, '64.
Estes George H.	25	July 29, '62	Missing in action, June 9, '64.
Ferguson George P.	20	Feb. 12, '62	To re-enlist, Feb. 21, '64.
Ferguson George P.	22	Feb. 22, '64	Disability, Oct. 28, '64.
Ferguson Samuel A.	22	Dec. 26, '61	To re-enlist, Dec. 28, '63.
Ferguson Samuel A.	24	Dec. 29, '63	Expiration of service, in Co. I, Aug. 16, '65.
Foote John C.	27	July 22, '62	Expiration of service, July 8, '64.
Frye Alfred	32	July 30, '62	To re-enlist, Dec. 30, '63.
Frye Alfred	34	Dec. 31, '63	Died at Andersonville, Dec. 26, '64.
Getchell George F.	29	Aug. 6, '62	Expiration of service, July 8, '64.
Getchell James A.	30	Feb. 24, '62	Expiration of service, Feb. 24, '65.
Goldthwaite Luther M.	21	July 5, '61	To re-enlist, Dec. 17, '63.
Goldthwaite Luther M.	23	Dec. 18, '63	Expiration of service in Co. I, Aug. 16, '65.
Goss Samuel I. T.	23	July 5, '61	To re-enlist, Dec. 28, '63.
Goss Samuel I. T.	25	Dec. 29, '63	Expiration of service in Co. I, Aug. 16, '65.
Grimes Charles H.	23	July 5, '61	Disability, May 20, '62.
Hobbs George	40	"	To re-enlist, Dec. 17, '63.
Jeffs James M.	43	"	Disability, July 5, '62.
Jewett Lewis T.	24	"	Expiration of service, July 8, '64.
Kehew Samuel B.	31	"	Disability, Nov. 7, '62.
Lee John W.	19	"	Disability, Jan. 8, '63.
Low Cornelius B.	21	"	Transferred Jan. 10, '64, V. R. Corps.
Mahoney John W.	18	"	To re-enlist Jan. 4, '64.

PATRIOTS OF SALEM.

NAMES AND RANK.	AGE	DATE OF MUSTER.	TERMINATION OF SERVICE, &c.
Mahoney John W.	20	Jan 5, '64	Expiration of service in Co. I, Aug. 16, '65.
Melcher George P.	20	July 5, '61	Disability, July 15, '62
Melcher John E.	31	"	" Feb. 9, '63
Morris James	40	"	" Jan. 8, '73
Nichols Benjamin C.	22	"	Expiration of service (absent sick,) July 8, '63
Noland Thomas	18	"	Disability, Nov. 1, '61
Norcross Orlando W.	21	"	Expiration of service, July 8, '64
Palmer Charles W.	26	"	Expiration of service, (absent sick,) July 8, '64
Pitman Nathaniel F.	31	July 24, '62	Died of wounds at Washington D. C. Sept. 12. '64.
Pulsifer Nathaniel F.	27	July 19, '62	To Re-enlist March 9, '64.
Pulsifer Nathaniel F.	29	March 10, '64	Died of dis. at Fairfax, Va., Nov 22, '64
Ragan Michael	19	Feb. 20, '62	To Re-enlist Feb 24, '64.
Reeves Edward	32	July 5, '61	Expiration of service, (absent sick) July 8, '64
Reeves William H.	32	"	Died of dis., Fort Albany, Va., Dec. 1, '61.
Sawyer Caleb	18	"	Expiration of service, July 8, '64.
Sawyer Nathaniel	24	"	Transferred Jan. 11, '64 to V. R. Corps.
Shaw John	24	July 23, '62	To Re-enlist Feb. 28, '64.
Skinner Emery B.	19	July 5, '61	Expiration of service, July 8, '64.
Smith Jonathan C.	37	"	" "
Smith John	29	Feb. 29, '64	Expiration of service, Co. I. Aug. 16, '65
Smith William A.	25	July 19, '62	To Re-enlist March 10, '64.
Smith William A.	27	March 10, '64	Expiration of service, Co. I, Aug. 16, '65
Smith William	23	Aug. 2, '62	Disability Feb. 15, '63.
Stickney George A.	19	July 5, '61	" Jan. 14, '63.
Teague Robert	30	"	Expiration of service, July 8, '64.
Thomas Stephen W.	20	Feb. 14, '62	To Re-enlist Feb. 28, '64.
Thomas Stephen W.	22	Feb. 29, '64	Expiration of service, Co. I, Aug. 16, '65
Tibbetts William R.	30	Jan. 16, '62	To Re-enlist Jan. 28, '64
Tibbetts William R.	32	Jan. 28, 64	Expiration of service, Co. I. Aug. 16, '65
Toby Stephen W.	19	Jan. 5, '61	Deserted May 27, '62.
Towne Samuel	25	Jan. 17. '62	Disability Jan. 14, '63.
Turner James H. Jr.	22	Aug. 5, '62	Disability Jan. 14, '63.
Upton Robert	19	July 5, '61	Expiration of service, July 8, '64.
Walton Edward A.	28	"	" "
Wellman George O.	18	"	To Re-enlist Dec. 15, '63.
Wellman George O.	20	Dec. 16, '63	Expiration of service, Co. I Aug. 16, '65
Wheeler Michael	32	March 1, '64	Died at Washington D. C. Aug. 1 '64
Williams John H.	18	July 5, '61	To Re-enlist Feb. 15, '64.
Wilkins Michael C.	30	Aug. 5, '62	Expiration of service, July 8, '64.
Wilson Richard M.	23	July 5, '61	" "

Company E.

Lakeman Nathan, Q. M. Sergt.	28	Jan. 2, '64	Supernumerary, July 31, '65.

PRIVATES.

Bailey Theron	21	Aug. 30, '64	Expiration of servce June 4, '65.
Bullock Atwood C.	22	" 31, "	Expiration of service, June 13, '65.
Currier Charles W.	20	Nov. 25, '63	Expiration of service July 31, '65.
Kellogg Fred B.	20	" 28, '63	Disability July 31, '65.
Lakeman Nathan	26	Jan. 1, '62	To Re-enlist Jan. 2, '64.

NAMES AND RANK.	AGE.	DATE OF MUSTER.	TERMINATION OF SERVICE, &C.
Noble Alexander J.	21	Aug. 31, '64	Expiration of service, June 4, '65.
Roberts William H.	32	Nov. 6, '63	Expiration of service, Co. A, Aug. 16, '65.

Company F.

NAMES AND RANK.	AGE.	DATE OF MUSTER.	TERMINATION OF SERVICE, &C.
Parsons George W.	22	July 5, '61	To Re-enlist Nov. 5, '63.
Parsons George W.	24	Nov. 6, '63	Killed at Poplar Spring Ch. Va., Oct. 2, '64.

Company G.

NAMES AND RANK.	AGE.	DATE OF MUSTER.	TERMINATION OF SERVICE, &C.
Bovey James G., 1st Sergt.	22	Dec. 30, '63	Supernumerary July 31, '65.
Webb John F. Com. Sergt.	22	July 5, '62	Expiration of service, July 8, 64.
Wentworth John H., Sergt.	22	Dec. 3, '63	" " Aug. 6, '65, Co. B
Deland Alfred N., Corp.	29	July 26, '62	" " July 8, '64.
Russell Martin V. B., Musician.	25	" 5, '61	" "
Young Aaron C., Artificer.	31	Aug. 6, '62	" "
PRIVATES.			
Avery John W. C.	27	July 30, '62	Died at Andersonville, Ga. July 25, '64
Baker William H.	28	Aug. 4, '62	Transferred to V. R. C. Jan. 11, '64.
Bartlett Calvin	26	" 8, "	Expiration of service, July 8, '64.
Bovey James G.	19	" 5, "	To Re-enlist Dec. 29, '63.
Bray Parker	31	Nov. 16, '63	Disability—June 14, '65.
Buxton Alonzo D.	28	July 24, '62	Expiration of service, July 8, '64.
Buxton John H.	23	Aug. 9, "	" "
Buxton Thomas	35	" 5, "	Died at Andersonville, Ga. Aug. 5, '64.
Cottle Alfred	29	July 29, "	Expiration of service, July 8, '64.
Cottrell William A.	28	Aug. 6, "	" "
Farley Charles	33	June 22, '63	" " Co. B, Aug. 16, '65
Fillebrown Charles C.	28	July 21, '62	" " July 8, '64.
Full William L.	36	Aug. 9, "	" "
Getchell Stephen O.	33	July 24, "	" "
Gorman Thomas	23	Aug. 6, "	" "
Harris John P.	25	" 4, "	" "
Hayward Charles E.	32	July 31, "	" "
Hayford William B.	40	Aug. 5, "	" "
Johnson William B. F.	28	" 1, "	" "
Kingsley William P.	25	July 5, "	" "
Luscomb William L.	27	" 1, "	" "
Monarch George H.	28	" 5, '61	" "
Needham James F.	23	Aug. 4, '62	" "
Osborn Josiah B.	28	"	" "
Parshley Nathaniel D.	21	July 5, '61	To Re-enlist Jan. 2, '64.
Purbeck John H.	26	" 17, '62	Disability—Aug. 22, '63.
Peirce Charles H.	32	Aug. 6, '62	Expiration of service, July 8, '64.
Pitman William H.	44	" 5, "	" "
Pulsifer Charles A.	20	" 1, "	" "
Sanborn Horace E.	26	" 15, "	" "
Skerry Edward S.	33	"	" "
Soley Nathaniel	28	" 28, "	" "
Staples Elias C.	41	Nov. 20, '63	Killed at Spottsylvania, Va., May 19, '64
Teague Thomas A.	37	Aug. 5, '62	Disability—Feb. 26, '63.
Tucker Henry G.	24	" 6, "	Expiration of service, July 8, '64.

PATRIOTS OF SALEM. 31

NAMES AND RANK.	AGE.	DATE OF MUSTER.	TERMINATION OF SERVICE, &C.
Watts Richard	20	July 5, '61	Disability—Dec. 14, '61
Watts Richard	21	" 21, '62	Expiration of service, July 8, '64.
Wenthworth John H.	18	" 5, '61	To Re-enlist Dec. 3, '63.

Company H.

Farmer George S. Sergt.	26	Jan. 2, '64	Died at Andersonville, Ga. Sept. 10, '64
Cocklin John J., Corp.	18	Dec. 7, '63	Supernumerary July 31, '65.

PRIVATE.

Russell George F.	28	July 29, '62	Expiration of service, July 8, '64.

Company I.

Plummer George, Sergt.	20	July 5, '61	Expiration of service, July 8, '64.
Wilkins Albert, 2nd Sergt.	36	Jan. 29, '64	Supernumerary July 31, '65.
Musgrave Peter, Corp.	21	July 5, '61	Killed at Petersburg, Va. June 16, '64.

PRIVATES.

Bassett Robert C.	26	" 19, '62	Died at Andersonville, Ga. Sept. 15, '64
Buckley Bartholemew S.	19	" 5, '61	Expiration of service, May 16, '65.
Buckley Patrick	22	"	Exchanged Prisoner of War, Jan 25, '65
Burrill Francis A.	19	"	To Re-enlist Feb. 9, '64.
Burrill Francis A.	21	Feb. 10, '64	Expiration of service, Aug. 16, '65.
Chambers John W.	22	Aug. 4, '62	Exchanged Pris. of War, Feb. 1, '65.
Dresser Charles F.	23	July 5, '61	To Re-enlist Dec. 6, '63.
Dresser Charles F.	25	Dec. 7, '63	Died at City Point, Va., Nov. 15, '64.
Fleet George E.	30	July 5, '61	To Re-enlist Dec. 6, '63.
Frothingham John F.	30	" 30, '62	Expiration of service, July 8, '64.
Green Joseph H.	29	Aug. 6, '62	Died at Annapolis, Md., Dec. 10, '64.
Haskell William H.	40	" 5, "	Disability—Oct. 8, '63.
Helt Benjamin G.	34	" "	Expiration of service, March 15, '65.
McGordis Charles	20	July 5. '61	Died of wounds, at City Point, Va., June 24, '64.
Murray George	23	" 28, '62	Expiration of service, July 5. '64.
Pitts Albert W.	21	" 5, '61	To Re-enlist Feb. 10, '64.
Pitts Albert W.	23	Feb. 11, '64	Deserted Oct. 26, '64.
Sheehan Timothy	21	Aug. 4, '62	Expiration of service, July 8, '64.
Wilkins Albert 2nd	34	" 6, "	To Re-enlist Jan. 28, '64.

Company K.

Bradley John	31	Aug. 1, '62	Died of wounds, at Salem, June 20, '64.
Conner Patrick	30	"	Expiration of service, July 8, '64.
Davis George A.	32	July 29, "	" "
Tibbetts George F.	34	Aug. 5, "	" "
Welch John	25	" 1, "	" "

Company L.

NAMES AND RANK.	AGE.	DATE OF MUSTER.	TERMINATION OF SERVICE, &c.
Frothingham Gustavus, Corp.	27	Feb. 22, '64	Died of wounds, at Petersburg, Va., June 24, '64.
Logan Jeremiah, Corp.	23	"	Expiration of service in Co. A, Aug. 16, '65.

PRIVATES.

NAMES AND RANK.	AGE.	DATE OF MUSTER.	TERMINATION OF SERVICE, &c.
Call George A.	21	Feb. 25, '62	To Re-enlist March 16, '64.
Call George A.	23	March 17, '64	Expiration of service, Co. A, Aug. 16, '65.
Coney Charles W.	35	July 18, '62	Died at Andersonville, Ga. Aug. 8, '64.
Cross George W.	22	Feb. 28, "	To Re-enlist Feb. 29, '64.
Cross George W.	24	" 29, '64	Died at Andersonville, Ga. July 17, '64.
Derby Charles W.	32	March 1, '62	To Re-enlist March 27, '64.
Derby Charles W.	34	" 28, '64	Expiration of service, in Co. A, Aug. 16, '65.
Frothingham Gustavus	25	Feb 21, '62	To Re-enlist Feb. 21, '64
Grimes Oliver	45	" 24, '62	Disability in Co. E. July 15, '62
Hancock John E.	18	March 19, '62	To Re-enlist March 20, '64.
Hancock John E.	20	March 21, '64	Expiration of service in Co. A, Aug. 16, '65.
Logan Jeremiah	21	Feb. 20, '62	To Re-enlist, Feb. 21, '64.
Meady Albert C.	18	March 3, '62	Expiration of service, Co. E. March 7, '65.
Pendergast Thomas	30	March 24, '62	To Re-enlist March 13, '64.
Pendergast Thomas	32	March 14, '64	Died at Salem, Mass.. May 20, '65.
Porter William T.	18	" 3, '62	To Re-enlist March 10, '64.
Shutes John D.	37	Jan. 6, '64	Expiration of service, Co. A, Aug. 25, '65.

Company M.

NAMES AND RANK.	AGE.	DATE OF MUSTER.	TERMINATION OF SERVICE, &c.
Randall Charles W., Sergt.	22	March 24, '64	Expiration of service, Aug. 16, '65.
Fowler Samuel M., Corp.	23	" 20, '62	Died at Andersonville, Ga., Aug 13, '65

PRIVATES.

NAMES AND RANK.	AGE.	DATE OF MUSTER.	TERMINATION OF SERVICE, &c.
Bolton Thomas	25	" 12, '62	To Re-enlist March 16, '64.
Bolton Thomas	27	" 17, '64	Transferred to Navy, April 1, '64.
Gardner Horace B.	28	" 7, '62	Disability June, '64.
Holmes George H.	23	" 10, '62	To Re-enlist Feb. 28, '64.
Holmes George H.	25	Feb. 29, '64	Expiration of service, July 28, '65.
Leahy David	25	March 13, '62	Deserted April 4, 62.
Manning Horace	34	" 10, '62	Died at Fort DeKalb, Va., June 12, '62.
Manning William H.	21	" 3, "	Expiration of service, March 2, '65.
Randall Charles W.	20	" 19, "	To Re-enlist March 23, '64.
Towns Calvin L.	22	" 1, "	" " 10, "
Towns Calvin L.	24	" 11, '64	Died of wounds, at Washington, D. C. Oct. 18, '64.

Unassigned Recruits.

NAMES AND RANK.	AGE.	DATE OF MUSTER.	TERMINATION OF SERVICE, &c.
Brown James	38	Aug. 6, '62	
Carroll Peter	23	" 1, "	
Folsom Nathaniel F.	27	July 22, '63	

PATRIOTS OF SALEM.   33

Second Regiment Heavy Artillery, M.V., —Three Years.

NAMES AND RANK.	AGE.	DATE OF MUSTER.	TERMINATION OF SERVICE, &C.
Samuel C. Oliver, Lieut. Col.	35	Sept. 18, '65	Expiration of service, as Maj., Brevet Brigadier General.
Samuel C. Oliver, Major.	33	June 29, '63	Lieut. Col. Sept. 18, 65.
James A. Emmerton, Surg.	27	May 26, '64	Expiration of service, Sept. 3, '65.
Henry A. Merritt, 1st Lieut.	18	Aug. 17, '64	" "
Fred Grant, 1st Lieut.	30	Jan. 17, '65	" "
Fred Grant, 2nd Lieut.	29	Oct. 9, '63	1st Lieut. Jan. 17, '65.
Ephraim A. Annable, 2nd Lieut.	24	Jan. 10, '65	Expiration of service, Sept. 3, '65.
Joshua C. Goodale, 2nd "	28	April 26, '65	" "
Thomas F. Dodge, 2nd "	28	June 9, '65	Expiration of service as 1st Sergt, Sept. 3, '65.

Company A.

Leary Dennis	42	July 28, '63	Died at Andersonville, Ga., July 2, '64

Company B.

Daley Charles P., Sergt.	27	July 28, 63	Expiration of service, Co. C, July 13, '65
PRIVATES.			
Baker Benjamin	44	"	Disability—Sept. 19, '63.
Burgess Charles H.	19	"	Died at Newbern, N. C., Feb. 5, '64.

Company C.

Goodale Joshua C., Sergt.	26	Aug. 4, '63	2nd Lieut. April 26, '65.
Davis Jefferson R., Musician	18	"	Expiration of service, Sept. 3, '65.
PRIVATES.			
Dalton James	45	"	" "
Milward Benjamin F.	19	"	1st Lieut. 59th M. V., Jan. 25, '64.

Company G.

Linehan John, Sergt.	19	Dec. 9, '63	Expiration of service, Sept. 3, '65.
PRIVATE.			
Firth John A.	21	July 25, '64	Deserted, July 6, '65.

Company H.

NAMES AND RANK.	AGE.	DATE OF MUSTER.	TERMINATION OF SERVICE, &C.
Hutchinson William	34	July 29, '64	Expiration of service, Sept. 3, '65.
Knowland John B.	32	Dec. 7, '63	" " July 20, "
Phillips Benjamin A.	25	"	Disability—Aug. 14, '65.
Savory John	21	"	Died at Florence, S. C., Nov. 25, '64.

Company I.

NAMES AND RANK.	AGE.	DATE OF MUSTER.	TERMINATION OF SERVICE, &C.
Thompson William	27	Dec. 11, '63	Expiration of service, (absent sick,) Sept. 3, '65.

Company K.

NAMES AND RANK.	AGE.	DATE OF MUSTER.	TERMINATION OF SERVICE, &C.
Chamberlain Luther L., Lieut.	31	Dec. 22, '63	Expiration of service, Sept. 3, '65.
Converse Francis T., Bugler.	30	"	" "
Converse Josiah L., Bugler.	36	"	" "
PRIVATES.			
Allen Edward F.	23	"	" "
Brackett Warren	21	"	Disability—Feb. 20, '65.
Richardson Alfred J.	34	"	Expiration of service, Sept. 3, '65.
Shea Patrick	21	"	" "
Shirley John	21	"	" "

Company L.

NAMES AND RANK.	AGE.	DATE OF MUSTER.	TERMINATION OF SERVICE, &C.
Dodge Thomas F., 1st Sergt.	27	Dec. 25, '63	2nd Lieut. June 9, '65.
Downing Henry W., Sergt.	24	"	Expiration of service, Sept. 3, '65.
Pratt Lewis R., Sergt.	24	"	" "
PRIVATES.			
Adams George W.	39	"	" "
Gilley George S.	23	Dec. 22, '63	Transferred to Navy, April 15, '64.
Hayes James	27	"	" "
Mack William	18	"	Expiration of service, Sept. 3, '65.
Real Joseph F.	18	"	" " June 16, "

Company M.

NAMES AND RANK.	AGE.	DATE OF MUSTER.	TERMINATION OF SERVICE, &C.
Twomey Thomas, Corp.	33	Dec. 28, '63	Expiration of service, Sept. 3, '65.
PRIVATES.			
Flakefield Charles	32	" 24, "	Died at Kingston, N.C., March 10, '65.
Kezar George L.	28	" "	Expiration of service, Sept. 3, '65.
Landers David	24	" "	" " June 8, "

Third Regiment Heavy Artillery, M.V.,—Three Years.

Pickering John, Capt.	45	Feb. 11, '64	Expiration of service, Sept. 26, '65.
Parsons Joseph M., Capt.	23	May 28, "	" " " 18, "
Parsons Joseph M., 1st Lieut.	23	Nov. 24, '63	Capt. May 28, '64.
Leonard James, 2nd Lieut.	22	Oct. 29, '64	Expiration of service, Sept 18, '65.
Coleman Francis M., 2nd Lieut.	21	"	"
Luscomb Henry R., 2nd Lieut.	25	Sept. 27, '65	"

Company A.

Leonard James, 1st Sergt.	22	Jan. 10, '63	2nd Lieut. Oct. 29, '64.
Luscomb Henry R., Sergt.	25	" 24, "	" Sept. 27, '65.
Coleman Francis M., Sergt.	21	" 10, "	" Oct. 29, '64.
Kimball W. L.,	30	"	Transferred to Navy, Sept. 15, '64.
Morrissey John, Corp.	25	"	" " May 7, "
PRIVATES.			
Barnes Michael D.	35	"	Disability—June 19, '64
Cowley Richard	18	"	Expiration of service, Sept. 18, '65.
Gibson John F.	33	"	Disability—Sept. 5, ,64.
Hill Charles H.	18	"	Expiration of service, Sept. 18, '65.
Kimball Charles A.	30	"	" "
Kingsley John	42	"	Disability—Dec. 5, '63.
Marshall Robert C.	35	"	Transferred to Navy, June 19, '64.
Nickerson Ansel	27	"	Expiration of service, Sept. 18, '65.
Nolan Thomas	19	"	Disability—Aug. 10, '64.
Pratt William A.	21	"	Transferred to Navy, April 15, '64.
Sharp Thomas	33	"	Disability—Aug. 13, '63.

Company C.

NAMES AND RANK.	AGE.	DATE OF MUSTER.	TERMINATION OF SERVICE, &c.
Carr Thomas F.	21	Feb. 5, '64	Expiration of service, Sept. 18, '65.
Farroll John	21	"	Transferred to Navy, July 28, '64.
Fitzergerald Michael	26	"	Expiration of service, Sept. 18, '65.
O'Herron John	25	"	" "
Winters John	21	"	Disability—Dec. 12, '64.

Company D.

Pervier Benjamin L., Musician.	18	Oct. 19, '63	Expiration of service, Sept. 18, '65.
PRIVATE.			
Fairfield William	41	Aug. 14, '63	Transferred to V. R. Corps, Oct. 18, '64

Company F.

Rowell Thomas A., Q. M., Sergt.	23	Sept. 16, '63	Expiration of service, Sept. 18, '65.
Browning Clement A., Corp.	18	"	" "
Fisher Francis A., Corp.	21	"	" "
Thompson Darius N., Corp.	22	"	Deserted, July 9, '65.
Batchelder George H., Musician.	16	"	Expiration of service, Sept. 18, '65.
PRIVATES.			
Berry Edward A.	31	"	" "
Channell George W.	27	May 21, '63	Rejected Recruit.
Chipman William F. F.	18	Sept. 16, "	Expiration of service, Sept. 18, '65.
Clough William H.	31	"	Disability—May 30, '65.
Collins Cornelius F.	18	"	Expiration of service, Sept. 18, '65.
Fabens William P.	30	"	Died at Fort Wagner, D. C., Aug. 31, '64.
Hackett Harrison	22	"	Expiration of service, Sept. 18, '65.
Hanson Parker W.	18	Oct. 19, "	Deserted, July 1, '65.
Knights Jeremiah	44	Sept. 16, "	Expiration of service, Sept. 18, '65.
Lyons Charles H.	21	"	Writ of Habeas Corpus, Aug. 29, '63.
Simons Francis A.	25	"	Deserted, July 27, '65.
Southwick Elbridge M.	18	"	Expiration of service, Sept. 18, '65.

Company H.

Monies William H., Sergt.	28	Nov. 20, '63	Expiration of service, Sept. 18, '65.
PRIVATES.			
Evans William	27	"	" "
Foss John G.	22	"	" "
Lee John W.	21	"	Transferred to Navy, July 27, '64.

PATRIOTS OF SALEM. 37

NAMES AND RANK.	AGE.	DATE OF MUSTER.	TERMINATION OF SERVICE, &c.
Lewis Thomas W.	19	Nov. 20, '63	Expiration of service, Sept. 18, '65.
Manning Richard H.	18	Dec. 4, "	" "
McShea Thomas	21	Nov. 21, "	
Moran Frank	19	" 20, "	" "
Pray Joseph S.	21	" "	" "
Ramsdell Joseph R.	29	" "	" "
Ramsdell Peter A.	25	" "	" "
Ramsdell William F.	22	" "	" "
Sanborn Ed. D.	20	Dec. 4, "	" "
Shanley William	22	Nov. 20, "	" "
Stover Nathaniel F.	33	" "	Died at Salem, Mass., May 16, '64.
Symonds Ed. A.	21	" "	Expiration of service, Sept. 30, '65.
Waldron Joseph E.	22	Oct. 8, '64	" " " 18, "
York Ed. W.	25	Nov. 20, '63	Transferred to Navy, July 27, '64.

Company M.

Swasey Lewis G., Sergt.	22	Aug. 27, '64	Expiration of service, June 17, '65.
Powers William F., Corp.	18	" "	" "
Walker William, Corp.	33	" 26, "	" "
Lewis Charles W., Musician.	33	" "	Disability—Jan. 3, '65.
Burgess William H., Artificer.	27	" "	Expiration of service, June 17, '65.

PRIVATES.

Breed Elbridge H.	22	" "	" "
Breed Otis J.	40	" "	" "
Chick Daniel	35	" "	Deserted, June 12, '65.
Gallucia Hezekiah A.	41	" 27, "	Expiration of service, June 17, '65.
Gray Everhardt	30	" 26, "	" "
Gray John	21	" "	" "
Taylor William H.	25	" 27, "	" "
Trafton Charles	21	" "	" "
Wilkins Ed. M.	22	" 26, "	" "

Fourth Regiment Heavy Artillery, M.V.—One Year.

Chipman Andrew A., 1st Lieut.	29	Aug. 18, '64	Expiration of service, June 17, '65.
Farmer George S., "		Sept 2, '64	Commission cancelled.

Company A.

Chapman Joseph R., Corp.	26	Aug. 23, '64	Expiration of service, June 17, '65.
Osgood Francis A., Corp.	21	" 19, '64	" "

PRIVATES.

Archer Rufus P.	18		

PATRIOTS OF SALEM.

NAMES AND RANK.	AGE.	DATE OF MUSTER.	TERMINATION OF SERVICE, &c.
Brennan Michael	22	Aug. 23, '64	Expiration of service, June 17, '65.
Cahill Bartholomew	42	"	Died at Dangerfield Hos'p Va. Jan. 22, '65.
Callahan John	21	Aug. 19, '64	Expiration of service, June 2, '65.
Chesley Edward A.	18	"	" " " " 17,
Cogger James	21	Aug. 23, '64	"
Donovan Timothy	21	" 19, '64	"
Gannon John	18	" 23, "	"
Harrington Philip F.	22	" 23, "	"
Kiernan Eugene	30	"	"
Lyons Patrick	24	"	"
Mahoney Timothy	21	"	"
Maxwell Adam	23	Aug. 19, '64	"
Mitchell William F.	22	" 23, '64	"
Munroe Isaac M.	23	" 18, '64	"
O'Brien Stephen	34	" 19, '64	"
Peach George W.	23	" 23, "	"
Peach Thomas S.	30	"	"
Regan Stephen	25	Aug 19, '64	"
Regan Timothy	26	"	"
Tobin James	24	"	"
White Francis P.	21	"	"
Whitney Samuel	28	"	"

Company M.

NAMES AND RANK.	AGE.	DATE OF MUSTER.	TERMINATION OF SERVICE, &c.
Abbott Benjamin F.	22	Aug. 22 '64	Expiration of service, June 17, '65.
Arnold Edward H.	18	" 24, "	"
Bigelow Walter R.	22	" 22, "	"
Farrell Edward	34	"	"
Huntress Charles W.	21	Aug. 22, '64	"
Mc Donald Philip	25	"	"

TWENTY-NINTH UNATTACHED COMPANY HEAVY ARTILLERY, M.V.,

ONE YEAR.

NAMES AND RANK.	AGE.	DATE OF MUSTER.	TERMINATION OF SERVICE, &c.
Chamberlin Garland A., Sergt.	23	Aug. 29, '64	Expiration of service, June 16, '65.
PRIVATES			
Nimblett John W.	24	"	"
Trainer Thomas	23	"	"
Twist Joseph C.	44	"	"

First Battalion Heavy Artillery, M.V.,—Three Years.

NAMES AND RANK.	AGE.	DATE OF MUSTER.	TERMINATION OF SERVICE, &C.
Pickering John jr., 1st Lieut.	-	Nov. 3, '62	Capt. 13th unattached Co., H. A., Feb. 4, '64.
Parsons Joseph M., 2d "	22	Jan. 30, '63	1st Lieut. 12th Co. H. A., Nov. 24, '63

Company A.

Pousland John H., Corp.	-	22 March 5, '64	Expiration of service, Oct. 20, '65.
Mansfield John R. Wagoner.	-	42 Jan. 26, '63	" "

PRIVATES.

Lawton George F.	-	21 Feb. 10, '65	" "
McCloud Alfred	-	18 " 14, '64	" "
McMahon Philip	-	29 Jan. 3, '63	" "
McNeil Michael	-	28 "	Deserted Sept. 25, '63.
Morrison George M.	-	18 Feb. 14, '65	Expiration of service, Oct. 20, '65.
Pousland John H.	-	20 March 1, '62	To Re-enlist March 4, '64.
Smith J. Jewett	-	38 May 30, '63	Expiration of service, Oct. 20, '65.
Washburn Horace W.	-	21 Feb. 7, '65	" "
Whittemore William W.	-	35 Jan 2, '63	" "

Company B.

Gardner Abel, Corp.	-	26 Jan. 6, '63	Expiration of service, June 29, '65.

PRIVATES.

Aldrich Ed. M.	-	22 Feb. 11, '65	" "
Cunningham John J.	-	22 Oct. 28, '62	" "
Grimes Charles H.	-	25 Aug. 29, '63	" "
Grimes Robert	-	43 Jan. 7, "	" "
Phippen Joshua B.	-	33 " 17, "	" "
Pierce John	-	35 Oct. 24, '62	Disability, May 19, '64.
Pray Joseph	-	21 " 27, '62	Deserted Oct. '62.
Woodbury Levi	-	26 " 28, '62	Deserted Aug. 14, '63.

Company C.

Henfield James H., 1st Sergt.	-	23 April 22, 63	Expiration of service, Oct. 20, '65.
McCarthy Michael, Sergt.	-	21 "	" "
Kirkland James M., Corp.	-	29 "	" "
McCarthy John, Corp.	-	18 "	" "
Pinkham Charles, Artificer.	-	33 "	Died at Fort Warren, B. H., May 21, '64.

PRIVATES.

Adams Henry P.	-	35 "	Expiration of service, Oct. 20, '65.
Babcock John H.	-	29 "	Deserted Sept. 19, '65.

NAMES AND RANK.	AGE.	DATE OF MUSTER.	TERMINATION OF SERVICE, &C.
Carroll James	28	April 22, '63	Deserted May 7, '64.
Goodwin Thomas	43	"	Expiration of service, Oct. 20, '65.
Griffin John	25	"	Deserted Nov. 4, '63.
Loud Elbridge	28	"	" Aug. 10, '63.
Lundgrew James F.	31	"	Expiration of service, Aug. 20, '65.
Melcher George P.	22	"	" " "
Moroney Thomas	35	"	" " "
Nutter Horace	40	"	" " "
O'Sullivan Timothy	43	"	" " "
Osgood William H.	21	"	To Enlist in Navy, April 21, '64.
Peckham Charles	31	"	Expiration of service, Oct. 20, '65.
Rull Benjamin B.	33	"	" " "
Smith Henry	22	"	Deserted Oct., '63.
Teague Amos G.	34	Dec. 2, '63.	Expiration of service, Oct. 20, '65.
Teague William H.	25	April 22, '63	" " "
Tedder John T.	30	"	" " "
Veno Felix	25	Sept. 24, '63	" " "

Company D.

Cunningham Matthew, Corp.	21	June 6, '63	Expiration of service, Sept. 12, '65.
Manning William S., Corp.	26	"	" " "
Hutchinson John L., Artificer,	27	"	" " "

PRIVATES.

Cochrane James	23	"	Transferred to Navy, May 11, '64.
Cronan John	25	"	Expiration of service, Sept. 12, '65.
Desmond John	37	"	" " "
Fairfield John H.	24	June 6, '63	Disability, May 22, '64.
Gleason John	31	"	Deserted Sept. 1, '63.
Lorrigan Michael	22	"	Expiration of service, Sept. 12, '65.
Minnahan John	22	"	Deserted, June 18, '63.
Murphy James	39	"	Disability Nov. 23, '63.
Murphy Thomas 1st	18	Feb. 5, '64	" 21, '64.

Company E.

Long George	33	Feb. 11, '65	Expiration of service, June 24, '65.
McCarthy Daniel	19	"	" " "

Unassigned Recruits.

Baker Edwin D.	22	Feb. 14, '65	Rejected Recruit April 4, '65.
Peabody William	21	" 8, "	" "
Rogers Simonds	18	" 14, "	Died at Fort Warren, B.H. April 8, '65

First Regiment of Cavalry, M.V.,—Three Years.

Company D.

NAMES AND RANK.	AGE.	DATE OF MUSTER.	TERMINATION OF SERVICE, &c.
Brown Patrick	37	Aug. 6, '64	Expiration of service, June 27, '65.

Company F.

NAMES AND RANK.	AGE.	DATE OF MUSTER.	TERMINATION OF SERVICE, &c.
Henry Michael	23	July 14, '64	Disability June 5, '65.

Company H.

NAMES AND RANK.	AGE.	DATE OF MUSTER.	TERMINATION OF SERVICE, &c.
Ladd Daniel W., Q. M. Sergt.	27	Oct. 5, '61	Expiration of service, Nov. 11, '64.
Kelly Edward, Com. "	30	Dec. 26, '63	" " in Co. F. June 26, '65.
Keiliher James, Com. Sergt.	17	Oct. 5, '61	Expiration of service, Nov. 11, '64.
Kelly Edward, Sergt.	28	" 9, '61	To Re-enlist Dec. 25, '63.
Linehan Dennis, Corp.	22	Dec. 20, '63	Expiration of service in Co. F, June 20, '65.
PRIVATES.			
Bateman Charles	18	Oct. 5, '61	Killed, Rapidan Station, Va., Sept. 14, '63.
Henville William W.	40	" 5 "	Disability, Dec. 24, '61.
Ivers William	19	Oct. 5, '61	Disability, Sept. 11, '62.
Kimball William L.	28	Sept. 25, '61	" " 27, "
Linehan Dennis	20	Oct. 5, '61	To Re-enlist Dec. 19, '63.
McDuffee Hugh	27	Sept. 28, '61	" " 27 "
McDuffee Hugh	29	Dec. 26, '63	Expiration of service, (absent sick) June 24, '65.
Metcalf George W.	19	Oct. 12, '61	Expiration of service, Nov. 11, '64.
Ross Daniel M.	27	Sept. 25, '61	" "
Spencer Hiram B.	33	" 25, '61	" "
Taylor Thomas	24	" 25, '61	" "

Company K.—New Battery Cavalry.

NAMES AND RANK.	AGE.	DATE OF MUSTER.	TERMINATION OF SERVICE, &c.
Crawford James, Corp.	19	Dec. 29, '63	Expiration of service, June 29, '65.

Second Regiment of Cavalry, M.V.,—Three Years.

Company B.

NAMES AND RANK.	AGE.	DATE OF MUSTER.	TERMINATION OF SERVICE, &c.
Fessenden George	18	Feb. 7, '65	Expiration of service July 20, 65.
Ricker William H.	18	" 10, "	" "

Company C.

NAMES AND RANK.	AGE.	DATE OF MUSTER.	TERMINATION OF SERVICE, &c.
Converse Augustus W.	33	Feb. 27, '64	Deserted Aug. 9, '64.
Maxfield John G.	26	" 24, "	Expiration of service, July 20, 65.
Smith Henry J.		July 13, '63	" "

Company D.

NAMES AND RANK.	AGE.	DATE OF MUSTER.	TERMINATION OF SERVICE, &c.
Arnold Peter	38	Jan. 9, '64	Expiration of service, July 20, '65.
Chandler Benjamin F.	18	Feb. 15, '65	" "
Conners Cornelius	22	Aug. 27, '64	" " June 19, '65.
Saunders Charles	21	June 13, '63	Transferred to V. R. C., Nov. 28, '63.
Stevens John	22	Sept. 12, '64	Disability, June 24, '65.
Sweeny John	20	Jan. 13, '63	Expiration of service, July 20, '65.

Company E.

NAMES AND RANK.	AGE.	DATE OF MUSTER.	TERMINATION OF SERVICE, &c.
Buswell John H.	22	March 7, '63	Disability, July 15, '63.
Lord Thomas H.	32	Feb. 27, '63	Disability, Sept. 15, '63.

Company G.

NAMES AND RANK.	AGE.	DATE OF MUSTER.	TERMINATION OF SERVICE, &c.
Johnson John O.	44	Feb. 21, '65	Expiration of service, July 20, '65.
Melville Frank	20	Aug. 15, '64	" "

Company H.

NAMES AND RANK.	AGE.	DATE OF MUSTER.	TERMINATION OF SERVICE, &c.
Shine Cornelius A.	22	Dec. 1, '63	Expiration of service, July 20, '65.

Company I.

NAMES AND RANK.	AGE.	DATE OF MUSTER.	TERMINATION OF SERVICE, &c.
Bell William H., Sergt.	18	Feb. 10, '63	Expiration of service, July 20, '65.
Shortell Michael, Corp.	38	Aug. 22, '64	" "
PRIVATES.			
Hurley William	35	Feb. 10, '63	Killed at Waynesboro, Va., Sept. 28, '64
Leighton William	18	"	Died at Gloucester Pt., Va. March 26, '63.
O'Neil Michael	21	"	Expiration of service, July 20, '65.
Robinson William	28	"	Transferred to V.R.C. Jan. 19, '65.

Company K.

Jewell Charles C., Sergt.	18	June 26, '63	Expiration of service, July 20, '65.
Pierce William, Corp.	21	"	" "
PRIVATES.			
Blanchard William H.	22	Feb. 15, '65	" "
Heeney Thomas	25	Dec. 4, '63	" "
Poulson Lewis	30	" 16, "	Expiration of service, July 14, '65.

Company L.

Kelly Michael	21	March 28, '64	Expiration of service, July 20, '65.
Ricker Richard	38	Feb. 14, '65	" "

Company M.

Barenson Abram F.	21	Feb. 4, '64	Expiration of service, July 20, '65.
Lang Joseph	29	" 5, "	" "
Tucker Timothy	18	" 4, "	Disability, June 15, '65.
Welch Charles O.	21	" 8, "	Expiration of service, July 20, '65.

Unassigned Recruits.

Balger Patrick	34	Aug. 22, '64
Lang Joseph	29	Feb. 5, "
McGuire Charles	29	July 29. "

Third Regiment of Cavalry, M V.—Three Years.

NAMES AND RANK.	AGE.	DATE OF MUSTER.	TERMINATION OF SERVICE, &C.
Henfield Amos, Capt.	46	Feb. 21, '63	Disability, July 12, '64.
Pickman Benjamin, 1st Lieut.	35	April 24, '62	Dec. 20, '62.
Allen Pickering D., 1st Lieut.	24	Jan. 1, '63	Killed at Brashear City, La. June 2, '63.
Allen Pickering D., 2d Lieut.	23	Feb. 20, '62	1st Lieut., Jan. 1st, '63.
Henfield Amos, 2d Lieut.	45	Oct. 4, '62	Capt. Feb. 21, '63.

Company A.

Wilford John B.	40	Oct. 27, '63	Transferred to V. R. Corps.

Company C.

Wentworth John	45	Sept. 4, '62	Disability Nov. 15, '63.

Company D.

Young William A., Sergt.	35	Sept. 20, '62	Expiration of service, May 20, '65.
PRIVATE.			
Mulligan Martin	39	Oct. 19, "	Expiration of service, Sept. 28, '65.

Company E.

Burnham Joseph P.	43	Sept. 20, '62	Disability, Feb. 20, '63.
Daley Bartholemew	44	"	" Dec. 21, '63.
Mc Nulty James 1st	38	"	" Jan. 18, '64.
Sullivan Cornelius	32	"	Expiration of service, May 20, '65.
Welch John 1st	38	"	" "
Welch John 2nd	21	"	Killed at Winchester, Va., Sept. 19, '64.

Company F.

Batchelder Richard, Sergt.	42	Oct. 27, '62	Disability Nov. 20, '63.
Beston James, Blacksmith	25	"	Transferred to V. R. Corp. Co. D.
PRIVATES.			
Arnold James E.	44	"	Disability, Feb. 10, '65.
Britton John	38	"	" Aug. 24, '63.

PATRIOTS OF SALEM. 45

NAMES AND RANK.	AGE.	DATE OF MUSTER.	TERMINATION OF SERVICE, &c.
Burgess Charles H.	18	Oct. 27, '62	
Kezar Albert	20	"	Expiration of service, May 29, '65.
Lond Charles A.	21	"	To accept com., Sept. 28, '63.
Loud George B.	18	"	Oct. 26, '63.
Mallen Henry	18	"	Expiration of service, June 2, '65.
Murphy Michael	18	"	Disability, Nov. 27, '63.
Mevil Patrick	38	"	Transferred to V. R. C. April 22, '64.
Ryan John	26	"	Deserted Nov. 8, '62.
Swasey Thomas S. B.	18	"	" Oct. 27, '62.
Taylor William	30	"	" Nov. 3, '62.

Company H.

Taylor James	28	Oct. 27, '62	Deserted, Nov. 5, '62.

Company I.

Baker Barney	44	Aug. 8, '62	Transferred to V. R. C, July 1, '63.

Company L.

Batchelder Charles J., Sergt.	25	Oct, 22, '61	1st Lieut. July 14, '62.
Merrill Parker, Com. Sergt.	27	Nov. 2, "	Transferred to V. R. C. Co. K., March 1, '64.
Dowst Joshua W., Corp.	26	Dec. 2, "	Disability, June 30, '63.
West W. C., Corp.	18	Oct. 15, "	Promotion Co. L. Aug. 4, '63.
Brown Benjamin K., Wagoner.	29	" 21, "	Expiration of service, Co. L., Dec. 27, '64.
PRIVATES.			
Carpenter Isaac W.	23	Nov. 5, '61	Disability, June 11, '62.
Fitzgerald Terrence	30	Nov. 2, '61	" " 14, '62
Keating John L.	29	March 14, '64	Transferred to Navy, July 2, '64.
Tracy Joseph	18	Dec. 31, '64	Expiration of service, Sept. 28, '65.

Company M.

Day John M., Corp.	22	Dec. 31, '64	Expiration of service, Sept. 28, '65
PRIVATES.			
Powers Richard Jr.	23	"	"
Williams Thomas J.	33	"	"

Unassigned Recruits.

NAMES AND RANK.	AGE.	DATE OF MUSTER.	TERMINATION OF SERVICE, &C.
Foley James	26	Oct. 19, '63.	
Purbeck John H.	27	Jan. 2, '64.	Rejected Recruit, Jan. 7, '64.

Fourth Regiment of Cavalry, M.V.—Three Years.

Miller James, Capt.	19	May 8, '65	Expiration of service, as 1st Lieut. Nov. 14, '65.
Miller James, 1st Lieut.	18	Feb. 1, '64,	Capt. May 8, '65.
Miller James, 2d Lieut.	18	Jan. 5, '64	1st Lieut. Feb. 1, '64.

Company A.

Buxton Edward H.	29	Dec. 31, '64	Disability—Oct. 10, '65.
Collins John G.	34	"	Expiration of service, Nov. 14, '65.
Dickson Augustus	22	" 26, '63	" " June 1, '65.
Staten Alexander	28	"	Disability—Dec. 14, '64.

Company B.

Scribner Luther, Corp.	18	Dec. 21, '63	Expiration of service, Nov. 14, '65.

Company C.

Babcock John F., Corp.	28	Jan. 6, '64	Expiration of service, Nov. 14, '65.

PRIVATES.

Dean Charles S.	19	"	" "
Robinson Jeremiah	38	"	" "

Company D.

Farnham George A.	22	Dec. 31, '64	Expiration of service, Nov. 14, '65
Stone Joseph H. S.	18	"	" "

Company E.

NAMES AND RANK.	AGE.	DATE OF MUSTER.	TERMINATION OF SERVICE, &C.
Allen George W.	19	Dec. 31, '64	Expiration of service, Nov. 14, '65.
Grover John C.	18	"	" " "

Company H.

Gifford Frank	21	Feb. 8, '64	Died at Hampton, Va., June 29, '64.

Company L.

Burke Michael	21	Oct. 26, '64	Deserted, July 21, '65.
Butler Charles	21	"	" Aug. 11, '65.
Graham William	28	"	" " 14, "
Keene Charles	27	"	" " 19, "
Murray Martin	21	Oct. 26, '64	" " 17, "

Fifth Regiment of Cavalry, M V.—Three Years

Moore Thomas H., Saddler.	25	Feb. 20, '64	Expiration of service, Oct. 31, '65.

First Battalion Frontier Cavalry, M.V.,—Three Years.

Company B.

Holt Frank, 1st Sergt.	29	Dec. 30, '64	2d Lieut., May 13, '65.
PRIVATE.			
Pope Thomas S.	35	"	Expiration of service. June 10, '65.

Company C.

Estes John F., Corp.	18	Jan. 2, '65	Expiration of service, June 30, '65.

Company D.

NAMES AND RANK.	AGE.	DATE OF MUSTER.	TERMINATION OF SERVICE, &c.
Berry William H., Sergt.	24	Jan. 2, '65	Expiration of service, June 30, '65.
PRIVATES.			
Gallagher William G.	21	Jan. 2, '65	" "
Goldthwaite Warren P.	18	"	Disability—Jan. 7, '65.

Company E.

NAMES AND RANK.	AGE.	DATE OF MUSTER.	TERMINATION OF SERVICE, &c.
Meek Henry M., Q. M. Sergt.	19	Jan. 2, '65	Expiration of service, June 30, '65.
Austin Amos P., Corp.	21	"	" "
Lowd Jacob R., Corp.	24	"	" "
LeGrand Charles E., Buglar.	18	"	" "
Harris John jr., Saddler.	21	"	" "
PRIVATES			
Bennett George A.	20	"	" "
Blynn George H.	24	"	" "
Brooks Horace A.	19	"	" "
Hatch Thomas C.	18	Jan. 2, '65	" "
Manning Philip A.	19	"	" "
Perkins Charles	21	"	" "
Perkins Joseph A.	24	"	" "
Peterson Andrew G.	22	"	" "
Stillman Edward	18	"	" "
Symonds Charles A.	18	"	" "
Walsh William H.	19	"	" "

First Regiment Infantry, M.V.—Three Years.

NAMES AND RANK.	AGE.	DATE OF MUSTER.	TERMINATION OF SERVICE, &c.
Lee John R., 1st Lieut.	34	May 25, '61	Resigned, Aug. 3, '61.

Company A.

NAMES AND RANK.	AGE.	DATE OF MUSTER.	TERMINATION OF SERVICE, &c.
Smith John B.	24	May 23, '61	Disability—July 18, '61.

Company B.

NAMES AND RANK.	AGE.	DATE OF MUSTER.	TERMINATION OF SERVICE, &c.
Daley Jeremiah	40	Feb 12, '64	Disability—May 1, '64.

Company C.

Wiley William	22	May 27, '61	Disability—Nov. 20, '62.

Company H.

Moore John G.	26	May 23, '61	Disability—March 7, '63.

Company I.

Gordon George E.	30	Aug. 21, '62	Expiration of service, May 25, '64.
Johnson George	38	Oct. 24, '61	To re-enlist Jan. 4, '64.
Johnson George	40	Jan. 5, '64	Transferred 11 Inf., May 21, '64.

Company K.

Perkins Charles C.	20	May 24, '61	Expiration of service, May 25, '64.

SECOND REGIMENT INFANTRY, M.V.—THREE YEARS.

Cogswell William, Col.	24	June 6, '63	Expiration of service, Brevet Brig. Gen., June 25, '65.
Cosgwell William, Lieut. Col.	23	Oct. 23, '62	Col. June 6, '63.
Stone Lincoln R., Surg.	29	Nov. 7, '62	Surg. 54th Inf., Nov. 20, '63.
Stone Lincoln R., Asst. Surg.	28	June 1, '61	Surg. Nov. 7, '62.
Cogswell William, Capt.	22	May 24, '61	Lieut. Col., Oct. 23, '62.
Brown Robert B., Capt.	22	Oct. 23, '62	Resigned April 15, '65.
Phalen Edward A., Capt.	23	March 31, '63	Expiration of service, July 14, '65.
Mehan Dennis, Capt.	20	May 24, '64	" "
Hill Edwin R., 1st Lieut.	34	May 28, '61	Resigned Nov. 29, '61.
Brown Robert B., 1st Lieut.	21	Nov. 28, '61	Capt., Oct. 23, '62.
Browning George F., 1st Lieut.	25	Aug. 10, '62	Disability—Dec. 22, '62.
Phalen Edward A., 1st Lieut.	24	Nov. 9, '62	Capt. March 31, '63.

50   PATRIOTS OF SALEM.

NAMES AND RANK.	AGE.	DATE OF MUSTER.	TERMINATION OF SERVICE, &c.
Mehan Dennis 1st Lieut.	20	May 4, '63	Capt. May 24, '64.
Brown Robt. B., 2d Lieut.	21	May 28, '61	1st Lieut., Nov. 28, '61.
Browning George F., 2d Lieut.	25	Feb. 11, '62	" Aug. 10, '62.
Phalen Edward A., 2d Lieut.	23	July 13, '62	" Nov. 9, '62.
Mehan Dennis, 2d Lieut.	19	Nov. 9, '62	" May 4, '63.
Edwards Charles W., 2d Lieut.	30	July 3, '65	Expiration of service as 1st Sergt., July 14, '65.
Browning George F., Q. M. Sergt.	24	May 25, '61	2d Lieut. Feb. 11, '62.

Company A.

O'Hare Andrew J.	22	May 25, '61	Disability—Nov. 4, '62.
O'Hare Polonius	21	"	" Dec. 20, '62.

Company B.

Alton Samuel T.	21	May 25, '61	Died of wounds at Gettysburg, Pa., July 17, '63.
Blake Darius G.	21	"	Disability—Feb. 28, '63.
Gardner Benjamin B.	26	"	"
Green William R.	21	"	To re-enlist Dec. 30, '63.
Green William R.	23	Dec. 31, '63	Expiration of service, July 14, '65.
Greenough Daniel S.	31	May 25, '61	Died of wounds at Resaca, Ga., June 6, '64.
Ham Edwin	21	May 25, '61	Disability—Aug. 11, '61.
Pope Joseph	18	"	" Jan. 13, '63.
Reardon Daniel	27	"	Expiration of service, May 28, '64.
Wallace John A.	19	"	Died at Frederick, Md., April 9, '62.
Wilson Joseph H.	20	"	Disability—March 28, '63.

Company C.

Browning George F., 1st Sergt.	24	May 25, '61	Promoted to Q. M. Sergt., Oct. 9, '61.
Edwards Charles W., 1st Sergt.	28	Dec. 31, '63	Expiration of service, July 14, '65.
Mehan Dennis, 1st Sergt.	18	May 25, '61	2d Lieut. Nov. 9, '62.
Phalen Edward A., 1st Sergt.	21	"	" July 13, "
Stafford James M., 1st Sergt.	32	"	To Re-enlist Dec. 30, '63.
Stafford James M., 1st Sergt.	34	Dec. 31, '63	Expiration of service, June 26, '65.
Edwards Charles W., Sergt.	26	May 25, '61	To Re-enlist Dec. 30, '63.
PRIVATES.			
Appelton John L.	38	May 25, '61	Disability—Aug. 9, '61.
Bailey Edward A.	26	"	To Re-enlist Dec. 30, '63.
Bailey Edward A.	28	Dec. 31, '63	Expiration of service, July 14, '65.
Barker Benjamin.	44	Aug. 4, '62	" " May 28, '64.
Burbank Nathan P.	18	May 25, '61	Deserted, June 27, '63.
Carlin Samuel	35	"	Expiration of service, May 28, '64.
Corcoran John	18	"	Killed at Cedar Mountain, Va., Aug. 9, '62.
Daley Timothy	36	"	Disability—Nov. 21, '62.

PATRIOTS OF SALEM. 51

NAMES AND RANK.	AGE.	DATE OF MUSTER.	TERMINATION OF SERVICE, &C.
Emmerson Charles H.	19	May 25, '61	Killed at Winchester, Va., May 25, '62.
Fitzergerald Conrad	20	"	Expiration of service, July 14, '65.
Gardner Robert	40	"	Disability—Dec. 9, '61.
Hennessy David	24	"	To Re-enlist Dec. 30, '63.
Hennessy David	26	Dec. 31, '63	Expiration of service, July 14, '65.
Jewell Franklin	18	May 25, '61	Killed at Cedar Mountain, Va., Aug. 9, '62.
Joye Robert H.	24	"	Disability—Nov. 21, '62.
Kimball Palmer	21	"	" April 25, '63.
Knight Jeremiah	43	"	" Feb. 28, "
Langmaid George W.	26	"	Expiration of service, May 28, '64.
Larrabee William W.	26	"	Killed at Cedar Mountain, Va., Aug. 9, '62.
Preston John C.	19	"	Disability—Nov. 10, '63.
Quinn Joseph	19	"	Civil Authority, July 1, '61.
Rice William H. C.	19	"	Disability—Dec. 9, '62.
Staples George	37	"	Killed at Winchester, Va., May 22, '62.
Sweeny Morgan	18	"	Disability—Sept. 15, '61.
Voller Benjamin H.	40	"	" Oct. 14, '62.
Williston W. D.	20	"	Killed at Cedar Mountain, Va., Aug. 9, '62.

Company F.

Connors Jeremiah	29	Aug. 18, '64	Expiration of service, July 14, '65.

Company G.

Coleman Patrick	30	Aug. 10, '64	Expiration of service, July 28, '65.
King John	21	July 25, "	Deserted, Jan. 18, '65.

Company H.

McDonnell Philip	23	May 25, '61	Expiration of service, May 28, '64.

Company K.

Murray Jeremiah, Corp.	21	May 25, '61	Transferred to 4th U. S. Art., Feb. 14, '63.

Unassigned Recruits.

Crowford George W.	25	Oct. 15, '62	Never joined Regiment.
Junkee Augustas L.	18	Feb. 3, '64	Rejected Recruit, Feb. 26, '64.

Ninth Regiment Infantry, M.V.—Three Years.

NAMES AND RANK.	AGE.	DATE OF MUSTER.	TERMINATION OF SERVICE, &C.
Edward Fitzgerald, Capt.	35	June 11, '61	Resigned, Sept. 3, '61.
Timothy O'Leary, Capt.	30	Sept. 7, "	Expiration of service, June 21, '64.
Martin O'Brien, Capt.	21	July 29, '63	"
Timothy O'Leary, 1st Lieut.	30	June 11, '61	Capt Sept. 7, '61.
Philip E. Redmond, 1st Lieut.	20	Sept. 7, '61	Cashiered, Feb. 28, '62.
Michael Phalen, 1st Lieut.	21	Jan. 28, '62	Expiration of service, June 21, '64.
John Doherty, 1st Lieut.	22	July 2, "	Resigned, Feb. 12, '63.
Martin O'Brien, 1st Lieut.	21	Oct. 20, "	Capt. July 29, '63.
James O'Donnell, 1st Lieut.	21	July 29, '63	Expiration of service, June 21, '64.
Joseph Murphy, "	21	Aug. 4, "	"
Philip E. Redmond, 2d Lieut.	20	June 11, '61	1st Lieut., Sept. 7, '61.
Michael Phalen, "	21	Sept. 7, "	" Jan. 28, '62.
John Doherty, "	22	Feb. 10, '62	" July 2, '62.
Martin O'Brien, "	21	Sept. 26, '62	" Oct. 20, '62.
James O'Donnell, "	21	Feb. 8, '63	" July 29, '63.
Philip E. Redmond, 2d Lieut.	22	March 22, '63	Died at Hos. Washington, D. C., Sept. 17, '63
Joseph Murphy, 2d Lieut.	21	April 1, '63	1st Lieut. Aug. 4, '63.
Joseph Murphy, Q. M. Sergt.	21	June 11, '61	2d Lieut. April 1, '63.
Monaghan Joseph H., Com. Sergt.	23	"	To Re-enlist March 29, '64.
Monaghan Joseph H	25	March 29, '64	Transferred June 10, '64, to 32d Inf.

Company A.

Bellows John	21	Aug. 18, '62	Expiration of service, June 21, '64.
Brady Edward	31	June 11, '61	"
Deboa James	26	"	Disability—Oct. 29 '63.
Keating Patrick	26	"	Killed at Gaines Mills, Va., June 27, '62

Company B.

Remick Patrick, Sergt.	22	June 11, '61	Expiration of service, June 21, '64.
PRIVATES.			
Driscoll Timothy	24	"	Disability—Sept. 30, '62.
Keenan Michael	26	"	Killed at Gaines Mills, Va., June 27, '62
Powers Edward	30	"	To Re-enlist May 28, '64.
Powers Edward	32	March 28, '64	Transferred to 32d Inf., June 9, '64.
Tracy William	23	June 11, '61	Expiration of service, June 21, '64.
Whelan Michael	34	"	"

Company C.

Phiney Edwin, Corp.	26	Dec. 31, '63	Transferred to 32d Inf., June 9, '64.

PATRIOTS OF SALEM. 53

NAMES AND RANK.	AGE.	DATE OF MUSTER.	TERMINATION OF SERVICE, &c.
PRIVATES.			
Burke Richard	18	June 11, '61	Deserted, Aug. 27, '62.
Hurrell John	22	Aug. 22, '62	To Re-enlist Dec. 31, '63.
Hurrell John	24	Dec. 31, '63	Killed at Spottsylvania, Va., May 19, 64
Phiney Edwin	24	Aug. 22, '62	To Re-enlist Dec. 31, '63.

Company D.

O'Donnell James, Sergt.	21	Aug. 8, '62	2d Lieut. Feb. 8, '63.
PRIVATES.			
Hanson John	29	Aug. 2, '63	Transferred to Navy, April 21, '64.
Hughes Edward	23	" 19, '62	" " V. R. Corps.
Healey Dennis	35	" 7, '62	Disability—Oct. 29, '63.
Kelleher John	28	June 11, '61	" Nov. 28, '62.

Company E.

Philip E. Redmond, 1st Sergt.	25	Aug. 14, '62	2d Lieut. March 23, '63.
Matthew Lynn, Sergt.	30	June 11, '61	Deserted Feb. 24, '63.
PRIVATES.			
Brady Patrick R.	24	Feb. 27, '64	Transferred to 32d Inf. June 10, '64.
O'Callahan Eugene	44	Aug. 18, '62	Disability—Feb. 23, '63.

Company F.

Michael W. Boyle, 1st Sergt.	24	June 11, '61	Expiration of service, June 21, '64.
Joseph Murphy, "	21	"	Sergt. Major, Sept. 26, '62.
Martin O'Brien, "	21	"	2d Lieut. Sept. 26, '62.
Michael Phalen, "	21	"	" " 7, '61.
Thomas Fallon, Sergt.	25	"	Expiration of service, June 21, '64.
Edward Geigle, "	24	"	" " "
John Lorigan, "	25	"	" " "
Joseph Monaghan, Sergt.	23	"	Commissary Sergt., Sept. 26, '62.
Garrett Timmins, Sergt.	19	"	Expiration of service, June 21, '64.
Richard Carney, Corp.	24	"	" " "
David Cashin, "	24	"	" " "
Benjamin Hayes, Corp.	24	"	" " "
Patrick Tierney, "	21	"	" " "
Patrick Timmons, Corp.	30	"	" " "
John Doherty, Wagoner.	22	"	2d Lieut, March 1, '62.
PRIVATES.			
Broderick Dennis	30	"	Disability Jan. 5, '63.
Cain Patrick	18	Aug. 13, '62	Expiration of service, June 21, '64.
Callahan Patrick	36	June 11, '61	Disability—Oct. 30, '62.
Carey Hugh	21	"	

PATRIOTS OF SALEM.

NAMES AND RANK.	AGE.	DATE OF MUSTER.	TERMINATION OF SERVICE, &c.
Cary John	24	June 11, '61	Disability—March 13, '63.
Cashin Robert	29	"	Expiration of service, June 21, '64.
Clynes John	22	"	Disability—Jan. 30, '63.
Cochran Daniel	27	"	" Dec. 20, '61.
Connolly James	25	"	Expiration of service, June 21, '64.
Coogan John	33	"	Disability—Dec. 27, '62.
Creden Cornelius	20	"	Expiration of service, June 21, '64.
Cunningham Lawrence	22	Aug. 8, '62.	" "
Cusack Patrick	21	June 11, '61	Disability—April 13, '63.
Dailey John	30	"	Expiration of service, June 21, '64.
Darcy Thomas	31	"	Disability—Jan. 16, '63.
Desmond Dennis	25	"	Expiration of service, June 21, '64.
Dolan Patrick	29	"	Disability—Jan. 26, '63.
Donovan John	37	"	Expiration of service, June 21, '64.
Dowdell Charles	20	"	" "
Duggan William	42	Aug. 8, '62	" "
Farrell John	19	June 11, '61	Disability—Dec. 20, '61.
Farrell Robert	35	"	Killed at Gaines Mills, Va., June 27, '62.
Fitzpatrick John	23	Nov. 12, '63	Transferred to 32d Inf., June 10, '64.
Flaherty Thomas	25	June 11, '61	Expiration of service, June 21, '64.
Gannop John	19	"	" " as Gunning, June 21, '64.
Ganley John H.	22	"	Killed at Malvern Hill, Va., July 1, '62.
Graham William	25	"	" " as Gorham, "
Henessy John	27	"	
Hurly William	19	"	Died at Arlington, Va., Sept. 17, '61.
Jordan William	20	"	Expiration of service, June 21, '64.
Keating Michael	26	June 11, '61	Expiration of service June 21, '64.
Kelley Charles D.	18	Aug. 16, 62	Disability—
Kelley John	31	June 11, '61	Expiration of service, June 21, '64.
Kelley John	37	"	" "
Kelley John	38	Aug. 15, '62	" "
Kelley Michael	20	June 11, '61	Disability—Oct. 21, '62.
Kelley Simon P.	20	"	Expiration of service, June 21, '64.
Kennedy Martin	21	"	Disability—Dec. 26, '62.
Leary Timothy	35	"	" March 17, '63.
Lynch James	29	"	" Aug. 19, 61.
Lynch William	38	"	" "
McCarthy Daniel	24	"	April 8, '63.
McCarthy Patrick	23	July 22, '62	Expiration of service, June 21, '64.
McCarthy Patrick	30	June 11, '61	Disability—July 18, '62.
McFarland James	23	July 28, '62	Expiration of service, June 21, '64.
McMahon James	24	June 11, 61	Killed at Gaines Mills, Va., June 27, '62
McNamara Peter	25	"	" " "
Murphy Michael	22	"	Expiration of service as 1st Sergt. in Co. G, June 21, '64.
Neil Edward	24	"	Killed at Gaines Mills, Va., June 27, '62.
Norton John	19	"	
O'Brien Edward	24	"	Expiration of service, June 21, '64.
O'Brien John, No. 2.	19	"	Disability—Oct 30, '62.
O'Brien Thomas	24	"	" Oct. 7, "
O'Connor James	23	"	" Sept. 20, '62
O'Donnell Patrick	20	July 31, '62	Deserted in 1863.
O'Hara Patrick	27	June 11, '61	Disability—Sept. 16, '62.
O'Keffe Patrick	30	"	Expiration of service, June 21, '64.
O'Rourke John	22	July 26, '62	" "
Pendar John	35	June 11, '61	Disability—Jan 28, '63.
Powers James	23	"	Killed, May 31, '64.
Regan Dennis	25	"	Disability—Dec. 21, '61.
Regan Edmund	20	"	Died at Phil. Pa , Aug. 22, '62.
Regan James	22	"	Killed at Gaines Mills, Va., June 27, '62.
Rogan Cornelius	21	"	Disability—March 4, '63.

PATRIOTS OF SALEM.

NAMES AND RANK.	AGE.	DATE OF MUSTER.	TERMINATION OF SERVICE, &C.
Rogan William	21	June 11, '61	Died at L. I., Boston Harbor.
Rogan William	24	"	Died at Augusta, Ga., as Wm. N., March 14, '64.
Scully John	18	July 28, '62	Expiration of service, June 21, '64.
Shea Daniel	30	Aug. 7, "	" "
Sherlock Thomas T.	21	June 11, '61	Died at Bealton Sta., Va., Feb 18, '64.
Sullivan Patrick	20	"	Died at Andersonville, Ga., Sept. 18, '64
Tracy John	22	"	Died at Phil., Pa., Sept. 16, '62.
Twohig John	20	"	Disability—Aug. 18, '62.
Walsh John	19	"	Deserted, June 29, '63.
Walsh Patrick	26	"	Expiration of service, June 21, '64.
Whelan John	30	"	Disability—Aug. 19, '61.

Company G.

Driscoll John	40	Aug. 15, '62	Expiration of service, June 21, '64.
McGuire Thomas	32	" 21, "	Deserted, June 27, '63.
McHugh Patrick H.	28	" 7, "	Expiration of service, June 21, '64.
Murphy Christopher	27	" 16, "	Deserted, Jan. 21, '63.
Purbeck John H.	25	June 11, '61	Disability—Aug. 1, '63.
Walsh Martin	21	Aug. 12, '62	" April 22, '63.
Winter Lawrence	43	" 16, "	Died, Dec 6, '62, at Falmouth, Va.

Company I.

Cronan Jeremiah, 1st Sergt.	23	June 11, '61	Expiration of service, June 21, '64.
Green Thomas, Corp.	20	Aug. 7, '62	" "

PRIVATES.

Heaney Richard	32	Aug. 8, '62	Disability—March 25, '63.
Lewellen Thomas J.	18	" 6, "	Expiration of service, June 21, '64.
Mathews Lawrence	23	June 11, '61	Died of wounds, May 6, '64, at Wilderness, Va.
McKliget James	37	Aug. 18, '62	Expiration of service, June 21, '64.
McKormick John	33	" 8, "	Disability as McKormack, May 24, '63.
Spring Patrick	43	" 7, "	Expiration of service, June 21, '64.

Company K.

Cochlin John	34	Aug. 12, '62	Disability—May 12, '64.

Unassigned Recruits.

Burns John	32	Aug. 4, '62	
Burnham John	42	Aug. 7, '62	
Lynch Patrick	23	" 12, '62	
Smith Albert P.	20	" 13, '63	Disability—Sept. 17, '63.

Eleventh Regiment Infantry, M.V.,—Three Years.

NAMES AND RANK.	AGE	DATE OF MUSTER.	TERMINATION OF SERVICE, &C.
John F. Devereux, Capt.		Dec. 21, '61	Dismissed, Sept. 14, '63.
Thomas E. Bott, Capt.	32	March 2, '65	Expiration of service, July 25, '65.
Thomas E. Bott,	32	July 23, '64	Capt. March 2d, '65.
Patrick McGourty, 2d Lieut.	21	" 11, '65	Expiration of service, July 14, '65.
Azel P. Brigham, Musician.	29	Aug. 3, '61	Order War department, Aug. 8, '62.

Company A.

Batchelder John	18	Nov 18, '61	Transferred to V. R. C.
Johnson George	38	Jan. 4, '62	Expiration of service, July 14, '65.
King John	36	" 8, "	Transferred to V. R. C., Sept. 16, '63.
Miles Orrin A.	18	Jan. '62	Disability—Jan. 26, '63.
Southwick Joseph	20	Jan. '62	" May 20, '62.
Willburn James	34	Jan. 7, '62	Expiration of service, Jan. 8, '62.

Company B.

Gillon Hugh	20	June 13, '61	Died at Fort Munroe, Va., Feb. 10, '63
Glover Henry B.	18	Jan. '62	Killed at Williamsburg, Va, May 5, '62.
Lablair Louis	21	Aug. 13, '63	Expiration of service in Co. A, July 14, '65.
Moran James	32	Jan. 8, '62	Killed at Bull Run, Va., Aug. 29, '62.
Paishley Sylvester	18	Jan '62	Deserted, Aug. 25, '62.

Company C.

Millett William T.	19	Jan. 8, '62	Expiration of service, Jan. 8, '65.
Porter Charles	18	Jan. " 62	" " Dec. 9, '64.

Company D.

Cook Peter S.	24	Dec. 12, '61	
Cullen John	35	Jan. 7, '62	To Re-enlist March 26, '64.
Evans Daniel	28	Dec. 12, '61	Expiration of service, Dec. 12, '64.
Kayler Patrick	21	" 10, '61	To Re-enlist March 16, '64.
Seger John	35	Aug. 13, '63	Deserted, Sept. 17, '63.

Company E.

NAMES AND RANK.	AGE.	DATE OF MUSTER.	TERMINATION OF SERVICE, &c.
Millett Daniel	18	Jan. 8, '62	Died at Gettysburg, Pa., July 13, '63.
Sommer Sehan	21	Aug. 15, '63	Expiration of service, July 14, '65.

Company F.

Batchelder George H.	18	Dec. 12, '61	Disability—Feb. 4, '63.
Clarrage James O.	24	Sept. 2, '61	" May 5, '62.
Kezar Alonzo C.	18	Dec. 3, '61	" Aug. 15, '62.
Kimball James jr.	44	Sept. 2, '61	" "
Littlefield Daniel	42	Sept. 2, '61	" March 28, '63.
Rogers Benjamin H.	31	Jan. 8, '62	To Re-enlist Feb. 12, '64.
Rogers Henry N.	16	Dec. 3, '61	Disability—Aug. 15, '62.
Russell Albert W.	20	" 12, '61	Expiration of service, in Co. D. Dec. 14, '64.
Smith John	28	Jan. '62	Deserted, July 21, '63.
Tarbox Asa	21	Dec. 10, '61	Disability—July 9, '63.
Whicher Ira S.	22	Nov. 12, '61	Deserted, Oct. 11, '62.
Young Charles H.	18	Dec. 3, '61	Disability—Sept. 9, '62.

Company G.

Manning Peter	21	Jan. '62	Deserted, Sept. 6, '62.
Russell Albert W.	20	Dec. 12, '61	Expiration of service, in Co. D, Dec. 14, '64.

Company H.

Burns John	25	Dec. 12, '61	Killed at Williamsburg, Va., May 5, '62

Company I.

Shaw Orlin, Corp.	30	June 13, '61	Died of wounds at Gettysburg, Pa. Aug. 3, '62.
PRIVATES.			
Morgan Francis	24	"	Expiration of service, June, 24, '64.
Morrill Gilman L.	37	Jan. '62	Disability—Jan. 19, '64.
O'Connor James	42	Jan. '62	" April 27, '63.

Company K.

NAMES AND RANK.	AGE.	DATE OF MUSTER.	TERMINATION OF SERVICE, &C.
Allen Benjamin jr.	33	Dec. 26, '61	To Re-enlist March 16, '64.
Bott Thomas E.	29	Nov. 18, '61	" "
McGurty Patrick	18	Dec. 26, '61	" "
Poor Horace A.	18	Nov. 6, '61	" "
Trout Bradford H.	18	June 13, '61	" "

Unassigned Recruits.

NAMES AND RANK.	AGE.	DATE OF MUSTER.	
Brickley John	21	Jan. 8, '62	
Cochran James	22	"	
Cunningham Mathew	19	"	
Cunningham William W.	21	"	
Forbes Charles	19	"	
Sullivan Mathew	21	"	
Wells S. C.	18	"	

Twelfth Regiment Infantry, M.V.—Three Years.

Company C.

NAMES AND RANK.	AGE.	DATE OF MUSTER.	TERMINATION OF SERVICE, &C.
Allen James, Corp.	24	June 26, '61	Disability—Nov. 29, '63.
PRIVATE.			
Cummings Ed. D.	26	June 26, '61	" March 25, '63.

Company D.

NAMES AND RANK.	AGE.	DATE OF MUSTER.	TERMINATION OF SERVICE, &C.
Chipman Andrew A., 1st Sergt.	27	Jan. 6, '64	1st Lieut., May 26, '64.
Haskell Charles, Corp.	27	June 26, '61	Died March 10, '64 at Salem.
PRIVATES.			
Burnes Charles E.	21	"	Disability—July 11, '63.
Burnes George W.	19	"	Died Nov. 2, '62.
Casperson John P.	21	"	Killed at Antietam, Md. Sept. 17, '62.
Chipman Andrew A.	25	"	To Re-enlist, Jan. 5, '64.
Frye Daniel M.	19	"	Disability—March 6, 63.
Potter Francis B.	21	"	To Re-enlist Jan. 5, '64.
Potter Francis B.	23	Jan. 6, '64	Died at Washington, D. C., June 5, '64

Fifteenth Regiment Infantry, M V.—Three Years.

NAMES AND RANK.	AGE.	DATE OF MUSTER.	TERMINATION OF SERVICE, &C.
Richard Derby, 1st Lieut.	27	Aug. 6, '62	Killed at Antietam, Md., Sept. 17, '62.
Richard Derby, 2d Lieut.	20	" 1, '61	1st Lieut., Nov. 22, '61.

Company B.

Crawford Wallace	-	21 Aug. 5, '63	Transferred to 20th Inf., July 27, '64.

Company E.

McFarland Charles, Sergt.	-	26 Feb. 18, '62	Transferred to 20th Inf., July 27, '64.

Company F.

Long Robert	-	21 July 30, '63	Transferred to Navy, April 23, '64.

Sixteenth Regiment Infantry, M.V.—Three Years.

Thomas R. Tannatt, Col.	-	July 14, '62	Col., 1st Heavy Artillery, Nov. 18 '62.

Company A.

Allen Henry	-	36 Aug. 14, '63	Deserted, Nov. 26, '63.

Company B.

Sommer Sehan	-	21 Aug. 15, '63	Transferred to 11th Inf., July 11, '64.

Company C.

NAMES AND RANK.	AGE.	DATE OF MUSTER.	TERMINATION OF SERVICE, &c.
Kearney Peter	24	Aug. 15, '63	Deserted, Sept. 15, '63.

Company D.

McMahon John	18	July 12, '61	Killed at Wilderness, Va., May 12, '64.

Company I.

Hartman Charles	28	Aug. 15, '63	Deserted, Sept. 17, '63.

SEVENTEENTH REGIMENT INFANTRY, M.V.,—THREE YEARS.

Company B.

NAMES AND RANK.	AGE.	DATE OF MUSTER.	TERMINATION OF SERVICE, &c.
Leonard John H., Sergt.	29	July 22, '61	Expiration of service, Aug. 3, '64.
Mullaly William, Sergt.	19	"	Disability—Feb. 7, '63.
Leavitt Israel P., Corp.	28	"	" June 23, '63.
Buxton George jr., Wagoner.	24	"	Expiration of service, Aug. 3, '64.
PRIVATES.			
Bacheller William H.	24	"	Disability in Co. H, Nov. 29, '63.
Butterfield Hiram	21	"	Expiration of service in Co. D, Aug. 3, '64.
Cronin Patrick	31	"	" "
Desmond John	35	"	" "
Devine John	25	"	" "
Gallagher Thomas	23	"	Disability—July 22, '61.
Hart John	18	"	To Re-enlist Jan, 5, '64.
Hart John	20	Jan. 6, '64	Expiration of service in Co. C, July 11, '65.
Jones Alexander	26	July 22, '61	Disability—Dec. 3, '63.
Lucy Michael P.	24	"	Expiration of service, Aug. 3, '64.
Marley Richard	19	"	" "
McDonald Eneas	22	"	" "
McIntire Charles	18	"	Disability—Sept. 15, '61.
McLellan George	18	"	Expiration of service, Aug. 3, '64.
Mullaly Michael	24	"	Disability—Oct. 24, '61.
O'Shea Patrick	30	"	Expiration of service, Aug. 3, '63.
Ricker Richard	32	"	" "
Scanlan Michael	22	"	" "
Sheehan Edward	22	"	" "

PATRIOTS OF SALEM.

NAMES AND RANK.	AGE.	DATE OF MUSTER.	TERMINATION OF SERVICE, &c.
Stevens Daniel W.	26	July 22, '61	Expiration of service, Aug. 3, '63.
Tarbox Henry M.	22	"	" "
Thiers Patrick	27	"	Deserted, Nov. 29, '61.
Thomas George W.	18	"	Expiration of service, Aug. 3, '64.
Tucker John H.	42	Nov. 19, '63	" " in Co. C, July 20, '65.
Twiss Joseph C. 1st.	46	July 10, '61	Expiration of service, Aug. 3, '64.
Twiss Joseph C. 2d.	25	Oct. 29, '61	Disability—July 17, '63.

Company C.

Curran John	23	Oct. 10, '64	Expiration of service, July 11, '65.
Fox Lawrence	43	" 15, '64	" "
Martin William H.	18	" 21, "	" "
Robinson Harry S.	18	"	" "

Company D.

Fields Robert M.	35	Dec. 8, '64	Expiration of service, July 11, '65.

Company G.

Feldgen Hiram, S., Sergt.	26	July 22, '61	Disability—Dec. 7, '61.
Donavan Patrick H., Corp.	20	Jan. 5, '64	Expiration of service, July 11, '65.
Lewis Roland F., Corp.	20	" 6, "	" " in Co. A. July 11, '65.
Buxton Charles W., Wagoner.	29	July 22, '61	Disability—Sept. 8, '62.

PRIVATES.

Clough William H.	35	" "	" May 28, '63.
Donavan Patrick H.	18	"	To Re-enlist Jan. 4, '64.
Felt David H.	28	"	Disability—May 28, '63.
Huddle Benjamin	18	"	To Re-enlist Jan. 1, '64.
Huddle Benjamin	20	Jan. 2, '64	Expiration of service in Co. A, Aug. 9, '65.
Janes Edwin	19	July 22, '61	To Re-enlist Jan. 4, '64.
Janes Edwin	21	Jan. 5, 64	Expiration of service in Co. A, July 5, '05.
Leary Dennis	41	July 22, '61	Disability—Sept. 27, '62.
Lewis Roland F.	18	"	To Re-enlist Jan. 5, '64.
Maxwell Silas	42	"	Died at Newburn, N. C., Sept. 1, '62.
Mehan Mathew	17	"	Expiration of service, Aug. 3, '64.
Norris William E.	32	"	" "
O'Hare Charles H.	20	"	
Phelan Thomas	28	"	Deserted, Nov. 9, '61.
Phippen Abraham	30	"	To Re-enlist Dec. 8, '63.
Phippen Abraham	32	Dec. 9, '63	Died at Greensbon, N.C., June 18, '65.
Prime Joshua S.	39	July 22, '61	Disability—May 28, '63.
Quinn Joseph	18	"	To Re-enlist Jan 4, '04.
Quinn Joseph	20	Jan. 5, '64	Expiration of service in Co. B, July 11, '65.

NAMES AND RANK.	AGE.	DATE OF MUSTER.	TERMINATION OF SERVICE, &c.
Sharkey Charles	33	July 22, '61	Expiration of service, Aug. 3, '64.
Stone Benjamin F.	42	"	Disability—May 28, '63.
Willey George M.	18	"	" Aug. 2, '62.

Company H.

Cook David H.	18	Jan. 31, '65	Expiration of service, July 11, '65.
Kezar Alonzo C.	19	"	" "
McCam Hugh	30	Dec. 29, '64	" "
Murphy Hugh E.	21	March 3, '65	" "

Eighteenth Regiment Infantry, M.V.,—Three Years.

Company B.

Anderson Aust.	22	Aug. 26, '63	Disability—Dec. 8, '63.
Carlisle John	25	" 25, '63	Deserted, Sept. 16, '63.
Toomey John	26	Jan. 11, '64	Transferred to 32d Inf., Oct. 21, '64.

Company F.

Rock John	28	Aug. 25, '63	Deserted, Sept. 16, '63.

Nineteenth Regiment Infantry, M.V.—Three Years.

Arthur F. Devereux, Col.	26	Nov. 29, '62	Resigned Feb.'27, '64, Brev. Brig. Gen'l
Arthur F. Devereux, Lieut. Col.	25	Aug. 3, '61	Col., Nov. 29, '62.
William L. Palmer, Major.	26	April 8, '65	Expiration of service, July 28, '65. Capt., Brevet Col
Charles U. Devereux, Capt.	23	Nov. 15, '61	Resigned April 15, '63.
George W. Batchelder "	24	March 21, '62	Killed at Antietam Md., Sept 17, '62.
Henry A. Hale, Capt.	22	July 1, '62	A. A. G. Vols., Brevet Major, June 30, '64.
John C. Chadwick, Capt.	29	Sept. 18, '62	Major, 4th U. S. V., Feb. 26, '63.
John P. Reynolds jr., Capt.	24	Feb. 27, '63	Expiration of service, Nov. 5, '63 as 1st Lieut.
William L. Palmer, Capt.	24	April 16, '63	Major, April 8, '65.
William A. Hill, Capt.	22	Dec. 13, '63	Expiration of service, July 25, '64.
John C. Chadwick, 1st Lieut.	28	Aug. 22, '61	Capt. Sept. 18, '62.

PATRIOTS OF SALEM.

NAMES AND RANK.	AGE.	DATE OF MUSTER.	TERMINATION OF SERVICE, &c.
John Hodges jr., 1st Lieut.	19	Aug 22. '61	Resigned, June 19, '62.
George W. Batchelder, 1st Lieut.	23	"	Capt. Sept. 18, '62.
Henry A. Hale, 1st Lieut.	21	"	" July 1, '62.
John P. Reynolds jr., 1st Lieut.	22	Nov. 29 '61	" Feb. 27, '63.
William L. Palmer, 1st Lieut.	23	June 18, '62	" April 16, '63.
William A. Hill, 1st Lieut.	21	Sept. 18, '62	" Dec. 13, '63.
John P. Reynolds jr., 2d Lieut.	22	Aug. 22, '61	1st Lieut. Nov. 29, '61
William L. Palmer, 2d Lieut.	22	"	" June 18, '62.
William A. Hill, 2d Lieut.	21	March 21, '62	" Sept. 18, '62.
Converse Augustus W., Musician.	31	Sept. 3, '61	Order of War Department, Aug. 8, '62
Converse Josiah L., Musician.	34	Sept 9, '61	" "

Company A.

Call George A.	21	Aug. 28, '61	Disability—Dec. 13, '61.
Edwards William	48	"	Expiration of service, Aug. 28, '64.
Giles Israel	35	"	Disability—Oct. 14, '62.
Trask Edward	18	March 26, '64	Order of War Department, ' June 17, '65.

Company B.

Edwards William P., Corp.	23	Dec. 22, '63.	Expiration of service, Aug. 3, '65.

PRIVATES.

Edwards William P.	21	Nov. 29, '62	To Re-enlist, Dec. 21, '63.
Hayes John I.	18	Feb. 14, '64	Rejected, Feb. 28, '64.
Mooney John	19	Dec. 31, '61	Expiration of service, Dec. 30, '64.
Preston Charles H.	18	" 3, '62	To Re-enlist, Dec. 21, '63.
Preston Charles H.	20	" 22, '63	Expiration of service, June 30, '65.
Thomas James	23	" 3, '62	Died at Pt. Lookout, Md., Oct. 13, '63

Company C.

Wiley Moses	26	Aug. 28, '61	Disability—Aug. 1862.

Company D.

Warner Abraham F., Corp.	28	Feb. 16, '62	Died at Andersonville, Ga., Nov. 23, '64.

PRIVATES.

Estes William P. R.	18	" 13, '62	Expiration of service, Feb. 13, '65.
Freeze Noah L.	31	Jan. 28, '62	Disability—Aug. 25, '62.

Company E.

NAMES AND RANK.	AGE.	DATE OF MUSTER.	TERMINATION OF SERVICE, &c.
Clark John A.	18	Feb. 17, '64	Killed at Wilderness, Va., May 10, '64
Daley James P.	32	" 13, '62	Disability in Co. D., Nov. 5, '62.
Leary Timothy	26	July 26, '61	To Re-enlist, Dec. 21, '63.
Smith Timothy	39	"	Deserted, Aug. 20, '61.

Company F.

NAMES AND RANK.	AGE.	DATE OF MUSTER.	TERMINATION OF SERVICE, &c.
Hill William A.	21	Feb. 19, '62	2d Lieut., March 21, '62.
Horrigan Jeremiah	28	Aug. 28, '61	Expiration of service, Aug. 28, '64.

Company G.

NAMES AND RANK.	AGE.	DATE OF MUSTER.	TERMINATION OF SERVICE, &c.
Melden William R	20	Aug. 28, '61	Disability—Aug. 29, '62.

Company H.

NAMES AND RANK.	AGE.	DATE OF MUSTER.	TERMINATION OF SERVICE, &c.
Hitchings Abijah F., Sergt.	20	Dec. 10, '61	Disability—July 25, '63.
Warner George L., "	28	"	Died at Belial, Va., Oct. 18, '62.
Brown George A., Corp.	26	"	" of wounds at Fredericksburg, Va. Dec. 17, '62.
PRIVATES.			
Bailey Warren K.		"	Disability in Co. A., Feb. 23, '63.
Ball George H. A.	18	Dec. 10, '61	To enlist in U. S. Cav., Nov. 4, '62.
Bryant Enoch jr.		"	Disability—July 2, '62.
Carleton David	44	"	" Sept. 19, '62.
Cate John H.	27	" 3, '62	To Re-enlist Dec. 21, '63.
Cate John H.	29	" 22, '63	Transferred to Navy, March '64.
Chick William H.	23	" 10, '61	
Cottle Samuel	23	" 1, '62	To Re-enlist Dec. 5, '63.
Cottle Samuel	25	" 6, '63	Transferred to Navy, April 20, '64.
Driver Samuel	19	" 10, '61	To Re-enlist Dec. 21, '63.
Dunn James	29	"	Expiration of service, in Co. A. June 30, '65.
Goodsell Henry	18	"	Order of War Department, June 22, '64
Harrington Michael	19	Aug. 28, '61	Disability in Co. D. Nov. 20, '62.
Jarvis William H.	18	Dec. 10, '61	Dropped, Dec. 13, '62.
Lakeman Horace	21	"	Disability—May 24, '62.
Lewis Daniel S.	44	"	Transferred to V. R. C., 1864.
Macready Stephen	19	"	Disability—Dec. 8, '62.
McIntire Charles	18	"	" Feb. 4, '62.
Noyes Edward D.	40	"	Killed at Fredericksburg, Va., Dec. 13, '62.
O'Connell Timothy	21	"	To Re-enlist Dec. 21, '63.
O'Connell Timothy	23	" 22, '63	Killed at Blanford, Va., Co. B. June 19, '64.

PATRIOTS OF SALEM.

NAMES AND RANK.	AGE.	DATE OF MUSTER.	TERMINATION OF SERVICE, &C.
Parshley Sylvester	18	Dec. 10, '61	Disability—Dec. '61.
Powers Edward E.	25	" 1, '61	To Re-enlist Dec. 21, '63.
Powers Edward E.	27	" 22, '63	Transferred to Navy, '64.
Raymond Alfred A., jr.	18	" 10, '61	Missing since Dec. 13, '62.
Restell John	41	"	Disability—April 19, '62.
Restell John jr.	18	"	To Re-enlist Dec. 21, '63.
Restell John jr.	20	" 22, '63	Expiration of service, June 30, '65.
Roberts Samuel jr.	30	Dec. 10, '61	Disability—May 28, '62.
Rooney Peter	21	Aug. 1, '63	Transferred to 20th Regiment Infantry, Jan. 14, '64.
Simonds William	25	Dec 10, '61	
Smith Samuel H.	20	"	Disability—Dec. 3, '62.
Tareno Sareno	22	"	" Sept. 19, 62.
Thompson George H.	18	"	" April 8, '63.
Tirrell William	18	"	To Re-enlist Dec. 21, '63.

Company I.

Brown George O.		Dec. 10, '61	Disability—Oct. 13, '62.

Company K.

Quinn James, Musician.	18	March 26, '64	Expiration of service, June, 30, '65.

PRIVATE.

Thompson Edward C.	18	March 8, '64	Disability—June 7, '64

Unassigned Recruits.

Adams John H.	37	Dec. 2, '62	
Caras Lattara	35	" 10, "	
Chrystal Samuel	24	" 4, "	
Cunningham Thomas	21	" 5, "	Transferred to Navy, April 20, '64.
Eastley Alfred	27	Nov. 29, '62	
Enwright James	21	Dec. 10, '62	
Fairley Alexander	30	" 3, "	To Enlist in U. S. A., Jan. 31,'63
Fiske Peter	32	" 13, "	
Fitch John	22	" 2, "	
Goodwin George	23	" 1, '62	
Gray William	21	" 2, "	
Harrison George	25	"	
Hauseman William	21	" 4, '62	Deserted, Jan. 14, '63.
Homer George H.	26	Feb. 24, '62	
Jones William H.	30	Dec. 3, '62	
Jordan John	26	" 5, "	
Joyce John	26	" 2, "	
Miller Jacob	21	" 4, "	Deserted, form Co. S., Jan. 14, '63.
Mitchell William	23	" 2, "	
Moore Thomas	24	"	

NAMES AND RANK.	AGE.	DATE OF MUSTER.	TERMINATION OF SERVICE, &c.
Owens James	21	Dec. 2, '62	
Price Rufus	24	" 3, "	
Read William	20	Aug. 7, '61	
Roberts James	22	Dec. 2, '62	
Rollins William	26	" 16, "	
Ryan John	20	" 1, "	
Shearin Charles H.	20	Nov. 28, '62	
Smith John A.	43	Jan. 28, '62	Disability—March 23, '62.
Stenford Joseph	23	Dec. 10, '62	
Taylor Charles	21	" 9, "	
Waters Horace	36	" 4, "	
Wilson Thomas	26	" 30, "	
Williams George	24	" 1, "	
Wood John	23	" 2, "	
Wood John	22	" 5, "	
Woodden William	21	" 2, "	

TWENTIETH REGIMENT INFANTRY, M.V.—THREE YEARS.

	AGE	DATE OF MUSTER	TERMINATION OF SERVICE, &c.
Charles L. Peirson, 1st Lieut.	27	July 1, '61	Lt. Col. 39th Inf., Aug. 30, '62.
Pickering D. Allen 2d Lieut.		Nov. 25, '61	Declined Commission.

Company A.

	AGE	DATE OF MUSTER	TERMINATION OF SERVICE, &c.
Smith Henry J., Sergt.	23	Aug. 15, '61	Deserted, Aug. 26, in Co. E.
PRIVATE.			
Runey Peter	21	" 1, '63	Expiration of service, July 16, '65.

Company D.

	AGE	DATE OF MUSTER	TERMINATION OF SERVICE, &c.
Casey Daniel	38	Dec. 10, '61	To Re-enlist March 29, '64.
Evans James G.	30	Feb. 11, '62	Expiration of service, Feb. 11, '65.

Company F.

	AGE	DATE OF MUSTER	TERMINATION OF SERVICE, &c.
Chism William	25	July 11, '64	Expiration of service, July 16, '65.

Company G.

NAMES AND RANK.	AGE.	DATE OF MUSTER.	TERMINATION OF SERVICE, &c.
Hardman James	27	July 3, '63	Expiration of service, July 16, '65.

Company H.

NAMES AND RANK.	AGE.	DATE OF MUSTER.	TERMINATION OF SERVICE, &c.
Newell Charles O., Sergt.	20	Feb. 27, '64	Expiration of service, in Co. I., July 16, '65.
Warren William H., Corp.	22	Aug. 23, '61	Disability—Jan. 10, '63.
PRIVATES.			
Kershaw Samuel	30	Dec. 13, '61	" March 23, '63.
McCafferty Neal	21	" 31 "	" Aug. 28, '62.
McKenny Robert	32	" 20, '61	To Re-enlist March 29, '64.
McNamara Michael	27	" 23, "	Died Oct. 15, '62.
Smith William J.	19	Sept. 4, '64	Killed at Fredericksburg, Va., May 3, '63.

Company I.

NAMES AND RANK.	AGE.	DATE OF MUSTER.	TERMINATION OF SERVICE, &c.
Baker Robert	22	Aug. 7, '63	
Brooks Richard	28	Nov. 29, '61	Killed, June 30, '62.
O'Conner John	20	Dec. 4, '61	Disability—May 2, '65.

Company K.

NAMES AND RANK.	AGE.	DATE OF MUSTER.	TERMINATION OF SERVICE, &c.
Campion Patrick J., Sergt.	30	July 18, '61	Disability—Dec. 10, '63.
McFarland Charles, Sergt.	26	Feb. 18, '62	Expiration of service, Feb. 18, '65.
PRIVATES.			
Campion Edward J.	28	July 18, '61	Disability—April 4, '63.
O'Brien Thomas	24	July 24, '64	Never joined Regiment.

Unassigned Recruit.

NAMES AND RANK.	AGE.	DATE OF MUSTER.	TERMINATION OF SERVICE, &c.
Furbush Edward W.	26	Dec. 13, '61	

Twenty-Second Regiment Infantry, M.V.,—Three Years.

Company A.

NAMES AND RANK.	AGE.	DATE OF MUSTER.	TERMINATION OF SERVICE, &c.
Walton Joseph H., Corp.	27	Oct. 5, '61	Expiration of service, Oct. 17, '64.
PRIVATES.			
Brown George L.	31	Sept. 2, '61	Disability—Feb. 28, '62.
Calaracan Charles	45	Dec. 23, '63	Killed at Laurel Hill, Va., May 10, '64

Company B.

NAMES AND RANK.	AGE.	DATE OF MUSTER.	TERMINATION OF SERVICE, &c.
Frinan Kail	26	Aug. 27, '63	Disability—Jan. 12, '64.
Schwelts George	27	" 29, "	Transferred to 32d Inf., Oct. 26, '64.
Schilers Otto	22	" 28, "	" "

Company C.

NAMES AND RANK.	AGE.	DATE OF MUSTER.	TERMINATION OF SERVICE, &c.
Ferris Edward	28	Sept. 1, '63	Deserted, Oct. 13, '63.
Howard Fletcher	37	July 6, '64	Transferred to 32d Inf., Oct. 26, '64.
Kain John	35	June 30, '64	" "
Lehan William	20	" 20, '64	" "
Lynch Jeremiah	33	Aug. 31, '63	Died in Rebel Prison, Sept. 15, '64.

Company D.

NAMES AND RANK.	AGE.	DATE OF MUSTER.	TERMINATION OF SERVICE, &c.
Ambrose Charles	23	Aug. 28, '63	Transferred to Navy, May 2, '64.
Hall Thomas	21	"	Expiration of service, Aug. 23, '65.

Company E.

NAMES AND RANK.	AGE.	DATE OF MUSTER.	TERMINATION OF SERVICE, &c.
Husmann Johannas	20	Sept. 1, '63	To Enlist in Navy, April 25, '64.
Hytyes George	21	"	" "

Company H.

NAMES AND RANK.	AGE.	DATE OF MUSTER.	TERMINATION OF SERVICE, &c.
Bownar John	23	Sept. 1, '63	Transferred to 32d Inf., Oct. 26, '64.
McGuire Thomas	19	Oct. 4, '61	Transferred to 5th U. S. Art., Jan. 14, '63.
McShane James	19	Sept. 19, '61	Disability—Feb. 28, '63.
Morrison John	23	" 1, '63	Deserted, Feb. 27, '64.

Company I.

Robinson Edward L., Sergt.	27	Dec. 24, '63	Transferred to V. R. C., July, '64.
Plummer Lewis K., Sergt.	21	Sept. 6, '61	To Re-enlist Dec. 23, '63.
Plummer Lewis K., Sergt.	23	Dec. 24, '63	May 3, '64.
PRIVATES.			
Butman Luther C.	23	July 16, '63	Transferred to 32d Inf., Oct. 26, '64.
Daley James	20	Sept. 3, '63	Killed at Culpepper, Va., acc'y, Sept. 29, '63.
Farrell Owen	27	" 6, '61	Deserted, June 3, '62.

Company K.

Berry William R.	27	Sept. 16, '61	Disability—Oct. 22, '62.
Dalton James	42	" 18, '61	" Nov. 1, "

Unassigned Recruits.

Cook Frank	28	July 6, '64	
Crowley Jeremiah	21	June 20, '64	
Eck William	23	Sept. 6, '61	
Fairfield William	43	Oct. 17, '62	
Hostia Frederick	20	July 1, '64	
Roark Frank	28	July 6, '64.	Transferred to 32d Inf., Oct. 26, 64.

Twenty-Third Regiment Infantry, M.V.—Three Years.

Henry Merritt, Lieut. Col.	41	Oct. 24, '61	Killed at Newbern, N. C., March 14, '62.
Henry Merritt, Major	41	Sept. 25, "	Lieut. Col., Oct. 24, '61.
Ethan A. P. Brewster, Major	25	May 5, '63	Expiration of service, Oct. 13, '64.

NAMES AND RANK.	AGE.	DATE OF MUSTER.	TERMINATION OF SERVICE, &c.
James A. Emmerton, Asst. Surg.	28	July 31, '62	Surg. 2d Heavy Art., May 26, '64.
Ethan A. P. Brewster, Capt.	24	Oct. 8, '61	Major, May 5, '61.
George M. Whipple, Capt.	31	"	Resigned, May 2, '62.
Joseph A. Goldthwaite, 1st Lieut.	48	" 5, '61	Capt. & C. S. U. S. V., May 1, '63.
Charles S. Emmerton, "	19	"	Expiration of service, Oct. 13, '64.
Charles H. Bates, "	24	"	Resigned, Jan. 9, '63.
George A. Fisher, "	25	March 15, '62	Transferred to Signal Corps, Oct. 6, '63
George R. Emmerton, "	20	Aug. 20. '62	Resigned as 2d Lieut., Aug. 7, '62.
Richard P. Wheeler, "	28	Dec. 9, '62	Died of wounds, June 2, '64.
Charles H. Hayward, "	26	Jan. 10, '63	Sept. 28, '64.
John R. Lakeman, "	20	June 1, '63	Expiration of service, Oct. 13, '64.
Charles W. Brooks, "	23	Oct. 14, '64	Order of War department as 1st Sergt. June 7, '65.
George A. Fisher, 2d Lieut.	24	Oct. 8, '61	First Lieut. March 15, '62.
George R. Emmerton, 2d Lieut.	25	Oct 8, '61	First Lieut., Aug. 20, '62.
Daniel H. Johnson. jr. "	25	Feb. 9, '62	Capt. 40th Inf., Aug. 20, '62
Richard P. Wheeler, "	28	March 15, '62	1st Lieut. Dec. 9, '62.
Charles H. Hayward, "	25	Aug. 20, '62	1st Lieut. Jan. 10, '63.
John R. Lakeman, "	19	Nov. 1, '62	1st Lieut. June 1, '63.
John P. Ross, "	22	June 1, '63	Disability—July 29, '64.
William C. Cummings, "	33	June 2, '65	Expiration of service, June 25, '65.
Hayward Charles H., Sergt. Major.	24	Oct. 7, '61	2d Lieut., Aug. 20, '62.
Johnson Daniel H. jr., Sergt. Major.	24	Sept 23, '61	2d Lieut. Feb. 9, '62.
Driver Stephen P., Q. M Sergt.	31	Oct 8, '61	Disability—Jan. 24, '63.
Goodale Joshua C., Com. Sergt.	24	Sept. 28, '61	Disability—Dec. 9, '62.
Gardner Albert G., Pr. Mus.	15	Oct 19, '61	Expiration of service, June 25, '65.
Prown Henry F., Musician.	38	Oct 12, '61	Order of War Department, Aug. 30, '62
Terry John. "	32	" 14, "	" "
Wyatt Andrew J. "	29	" 12, '61	Disability—April 29, '62.

Company A.

Brooks Charles W., 1st Sergt.	22	Dec 3, '63	1st Lieut., Oct. 14, '64.
Lakeman John R., 1st Sergt.	18	Sept. 28, '61	2d Lieut., Nov. 1, '62.
Cummings William C., Sergt.	31	Dec. 3, '63	2d Lieut. June 2, '05.
Fowler William T., "	35	Sept. 28, '61	Killed at Whitehall, N. C., Dec. 16, '62
Hall Edward A., "	21	Dec. 3, '63	Expiration of service, June 25, '65.
Osgood Edward T. "	21	Sept. 28, '61	Expiration of service, Oct. 13, '64.
Ross John P., "	20	"	2d Lieut, June 1, '63.
Allen Horatio D., Corp.	20	Jan. 3, '64	Order of War Department, July 10, '65
Brooks Charles W., Corp.	20	Sept 28, '61	To Re-enlist, Dec. 2, '63.
Clynes Frank H., Corp	19	"	Expiration of service, Oct. 13, '64.
Hodgdon George R., Corp.	20	Jan. 19, '04	Order of War Department, July 12, '05
Rounds Edward H., "	20	Dec. 3, '63	Expiration of service, June 25, '65.
Smith Albert, P., Corp.	18	Sept. 28, '61	Disability—Sept. 11, '62.
Vinnah Frank, "	21	Jan. 3, '64	Expiration of service, June 25, '65.
O'Hare Chrles H., Musician.	18	Dec. 3, '63	" "

PRIVATES.

Allen Horatio D.	18	Sept. 28, '61	To Re-enlist Jan. 2, '64.
Austin Alden K.	21	Feb. 26, '64	Died at Newbern, N. C., Oct. 12, '64.
Brown Augustus	31	Sept. 28, '61	Died at Newbern, N. C., Aug. 24, '62.
Brown Ezra W.	19	"	Expiration of service, Oct. 13, '64.
Buffum George W.	21	"	" "
Clark William W.	26	Oct. 14, '64	Expiration of service, June 25, '65.
Collins Charles H.	25	Sept 28, '61	Disability—Sept. 12, '62.
Collins Edward A.	21	"	Disability—May 11, '63.

NAMES AND RANK.	AGE.	DATE OF MUSTER.	TERMINATION OF SERVICE, &c.
Collins George W.	20	Feb. 2?, '64	Expiration of service, June 25, '65.
Copeland George A.	18	"	"
Dodge Eben P.	18	" 17, '64	"
Foss John L.	24	Jan. 3, '64	Order of War Department, July, 12, '65.
Garney John W.	18	June 2, '62	To Re-enlist, Dec. 2, '63.
Getchell Charles L.	19	Sept. 28, '61	Died at Newbern, N. C., April 9, '62.
Getchell Edward E.	22	Nov. 4, '61	Disability—Sept. 12, '62.
Gillespie Joseph A.	18	Sept 28, '61	To Re-enlist, Dec. 2, '63.
Gillespie Joseph A.	20	Dec. 3, '03	Expiration of service, June 25, '65.
Goldthwaite Benjamin F.	26	Sept. 28, '61	Expiration of service, Oct. 13, '64.
Grant Edward H.	21	"	Disability—July 1, '03.
Hall Edward A.	19	"	To Re-enlist Dec. 2, '63.
Higley Gilman S.	24	"	Expiration of service, Oct. 13, '64.
Hodgdon George R.	18	"	To Re-enlist Jan. 18, '64.
Kinsman Joseph N.	18	Feb. 20, '64	Died at Newbern, N. C., Oct. 16, '64.
Linnehan Thomas E.	18	Jan 28, '62	To Re-enlist Dec. 2, '63.
Linnehan Thomas E.	20	Dec 3, '63	Expiration of service, June 25, '65.
McShane John	18	Feb. 25, '64	Rejected, March 3, '64.
Monroe Robert C.	19	" 15, "	Expiration of service, June 25, '65.
Murphy William H.	16	Jan 21, '61	"
O'Hare Charles H.	16	Sept. 28, '61	To Re-enlist, Dec. 2, '63.
Pollock David M.	21	July 24, '62	Expiration of service, Oct. 13, '64.
Pulsifer David F.	18	Feb 23, '64	Killed at Kingston, N.C., March 8, '65
Ricker Frances M.	19	" 20, "	Order of War Department, June 13, '65
Richards John H.	23	Sept 28, '61	Disability—Sept. 12, '62.
Schultz Carl F.	16	"	Died, April 24, '62.
Smith Charles F.	19	Feb. 26, '64	Expiration of service, June 25, '65.
Smith James E.	20	Sept. 28, '61	Transferred to V. R. C., Feb. 8, '64.
Smith Lorenzo	20	Sept. 28, '61	Disability—July 1, '63.
Stillman Amos	19	Feb 18, '64	Expiration of service, June 25, '65.
Stillman James H.	21	" 23, '64	Order of War Department, June 24, '65
Vinnah Frank	19	Sept. 28, '61	To Re en'ist, Jan. 2, '64.
Welch William L.	21	"	Expiration of service, Oct. 13, '64.
Wilkins George G.	18	"	Killed at Darry's Bluff, Va., May 15, '64

Company B.

Nimblett Benjamin F., Corp.	32	Dec. 3, '63	Expiration of service, June 25, '65.
Saunders Henry T., Corp.	43	Oct 3, '61	Died at Newbern, N. C., Oct. 9, '04.
Ayers Lorron "	27	Aug. 2, '62	Transferred to V. R. C., April, 17, '64

PRIVATES.

Call George A.	18	Sept. 28, '61	Expiration of service, Oct. 13, '64.
Flynn Thomas	30	Oct. 12, '61	"
Morgan Patrick	33	Sept. 28, '61	Died at Andersonville, Ga., Sept. 7, '64
Needham James	41	Sept 28, '61	May 30, '63.
Nimblett Benjamin F.	30	May 30, '62	To Re-enlist, Dec. 2, '63.
Pope Benjamin C.	20	Sept 28, '61	Expiration of service, Oct. 13, '64.
Prince George	40	Oct. 9, '61	Died of wounds, at Pt. Lookout, Md. June 9, 64.
Quinn Patrick	19	Sept. 28, '61	Expiration of service, Oct. 13, '64.
Shapine John	30	"	"
Williams Thomas J.	33	"	"

Company D.

NAMES AND RANK.	AGE.	DATE OF MUSTER.	TERMINATION OF SERVICE, &c.
Entwistle Thomas	35	July 14, '62	Disability—May 11, '63.
Hartwell William H.	19	Feb. 15, '65	Expiration of service, June 25, '65.
Hewitt Edwin W.	19	Aug 1, '62	To Re-enlist Dec. 2, '03.
Hewitt Edwin W.	21	Dec. 3, '63	Order of War Department, June 30, '65.
Patch John S.	23	Aug. 2, 62	Missing since May 16, '64.
Pitts Otis	42	Feb 15, '65	Expiration of service, June 25, '65.
Sweet Hartford S.	24	Aug. 2, '62	To Re-enlist, Dec. 2, '63.

Company E.

Blaisdell George E.	21	May 7, '62	To Re-enlist Dec 2, '63.
Parsons William D.	23	Aug. 5, '62	Died at Andersonville, Ga., June 22, '64.

Company F.

Snapp Philip J., Sergt.	37	Dec. 3, '63	1st Lieut. Oct. 15, '64.
Wheeler Richard, 1st Sergt.	27	Oct. 12, '01	2d Lieut. March 15, '62.
Carlton David, Sergt.	36	Dec. 3, '63	Missing since May 16, '64.
Davis Charles W., Sergt.	32	Oct. 5, '61	Expiration of service, Oct. 13, '64.
Daniels William F., Sergt.	18	" 22, '61	" "
Derby Putnam T., Sergt.	25	" 5, '61	
Fowler Philip M. "	29	" 1, '61	For Promotion May 30, '63.
Hayward Charles H. "	24	Oct 7, '61	Sergt. Major, May 10, '62.
Burchstead David W., Corp.	18	" 14, '61	Expiration of service, Oct 13, '64.
Carlton David, Corp.	34	" 1, '61	To Re-enlist Dec. 2, '63.
Carlton Joseph G. S., Corp.	24	" 1, '61	Expiration of service, Oct. 13, '63.
Emmerton James A., Corp.	27	"	Asst. Surg., July 31, '62.
Hiltz Jacob C., Corp.	19	" 10, '61	For Promotion, Nov. 8, '63.
Mansfield George S. Corp.	29	" 1, '61	Transferred to V. R. C., Feb. 8, '64.
Naigle Jacob, Corp.	34	"	Disability—March 20, '63.
Phippen George P., Corp.	19	" 10, '61	Expiration of service, Oct. 13, '64.
Robbins Louis L., Corp	19	Oct. 2, 61	Disability.
Winchester Silas, Corp.	20	Dec. 3, '61	Missing since May 16, '64.
Woodbury Josiah, "	21	Oct. 9, '61	Expiration of service, Oct. 13, '64.
Gardner Albert G., Musician.	17	Jan. 3, '64	Principal Musician, Sept. 28, '64.
Tarbox Samuel A., Wagoner.	26	Oct. 8, '61	Expiration of service, Oct. 13, '64

PRIVATES.

Arrington Benjamin F.	26	Oct. 14, '61	" "
Arrington James jr.	29	"	Disability—May 4, '62.
Austin William R.	19	Oct. 9, '61	Expiration of service, Sept. 28, '64.
Barnard Samuel jr.	24	" 17, "	Disability—Sept 28, '63.
Batchelder George H.	25	" 16, "	" Dec. 20, '61.
Bauer Anton	23	July 17, '62	" Sept. 14, '63.
Becker Peter	30	Oct. 2, '61	Expiration of service, Oct. 13, '64.
Brown Ezra L.	18	" 14, "	
Brooks Samuel H.	26	" 7, "	Died of wounds at Salem, April 6, '62
Chapple William F.	35	" 4, "	Expiration of service, Oct. 13, '64.

PATRIOTS OF SALEM.   73

NAMES AND RANK.	AGE.	DATE OF MUSTER.	TERMINATION OF SERVICE, &c.
Cook William L.	17	Oct. 9, '61	Disability—Oct. 13, '62.
Crocker Josiah M.	19	" 9, "	Expiration of service, Oct. 13, '64.
Derby Perley	30	July 28, '62	Disability—Aug. 7, '63.
Dudley Warren	18	" 19, "	" " 14, '63.
Edgerly Charles E.	17	Oct. 11, '61	Expiration of service, Oct. 13, '64.
Emilio Louis F.	18	" 19, "	2d Lieut. 54th Inf., Feb. 27, '63.
Farley James H.	21	" 14, "	Expiration of service, Oct. 13, '64.
Fischer William L.	26	" 1, "	" "
Glazier James E.	27	" 10, "	" "
Gray John H.	21	" 16, "	" "
Grosvenor Edward P.	29	" 30, "	" "
Hamblett Samuel H.	17	" 21 "	2d Lieut., 5th Battery, Nov. 28, '63.
Hinckley George O.	22	July 28, '62	Died in Prison, Oct. '64.
Lee Francis H.	24	Oct. 1, '61	Disability—July 19, '64.
Manning Albert E.	17	" 2, "	
Manning Joseph A.	19	" 8, "	Promotion, Aug. 14 '62.
Martin Henry	35	" 28, "	Expiration of service, Oct. 13, '64.
McCloy John B.	21	" 17, "	Disability—March 4, '62.
McDuffie Augustus	27	Aug. 8, '62	Expiration of service, Oct. 13, '64.
Morse Charles C.	24	" 8, "	Transferred to V. R. C., Feb. 8, '64.
Munroe Alexander A.	20	Oct. 9, '61	Expiration of service, Oct. 13, '64.
Nourse George A.	19	May 14, '62	Disability—April 27, '63.
Osborn Frederick M.	17	Nov. 7, '61	Transferred to V. R. C., April 24, '64.
Osgood George E.	19	Oct. 5, '61	" " Feb. 8, '64.
Perkins Eben S.	20	" 16, '61	Expiration of service, Oct. 13, '64.
Pinkham William A.	25	" 15, '61	Died at Fortress Munroe, Va., Sept. 30, '64.
Price William H.	21	" 9, '61	Order of War Department, Dec. 6, '62
Reed Benjamin A.	26	" 14, '61	Disability—Oct. 7, '62.
Roberts John S.	24	" "	" " Nov. 22, '62.
Rollins Abijah	28	" 16, '61	Expiration of service, Oct. 13, '64.
Sargent Charles O.	23	" 24, '61	
Scriggins Joshua C.	42	" 22, "	Disability—Sept. 5, '62.
Shaw Trown E.	25	" 9, "	Expiration of service, Oct. 13, '64.
Snapp Philip J.	35	" 9, '62	To Re-enlist, Dec. 2, '63.
Southard Samuel S.	30	"15 '61	Disability—Jan. 3, '63.
Stone George B.	21	" 8, "	" " Sept. 5, '62.
Swaney William H.	17	" 15, "	Killed at Drury's Bluff, Va., May 6, '64.
Symonds Nathaniel C.	17	" 11, "	Expiration of service, Oct. 13, '64.
Tibbetts Andrew R.	34	" 16 "	Disability—Sept. 18, '63.
Thomas Eli C.	19	" 4, '62	Died at Andersonville, Ga., Aug. 30, 64
Thomas Richard H.	20	" 16, '61	Disability—Sept. 5, '62.
Townsend William H.	19	" 23. "	Died at Point Rocks, Va., July 2, '64.
Trask Ames W.	17	" 11, "	Disability—Sept. 5, '62.
Upham Oliver W. D.	18	" 21, "	" " Dec. 29, '61.
Valentine Herbert E.	20	" 5, "	Expiration of service, Oct. 13, 64.
Wadleigh Curtis E.	22	July 28, '62	Disability—March 2, '63.
Waldron John	20	Oct. 7, '61	Transferred to V. R. C., Feb. 8, '64.
Waters Henry F.	28	" 17, "	" " April 20 '64.
Winchester Isaac	44	Aug. 28, '62	Expiration of service, Oct. 13, '64.
Winchester Silas	24	Oct. 14, '61	To Re-enlist, Dec. 2, '63.
Walcott Royal E.	29	" 8, "	Disability—Sept. 5, '62.

Company G.

Arnold James H.	18	Sept. 28, '61	To Re-enlist, Dec. 2, '63.
Arnold James H.	20	Dec. 3, '63	Expiration of service, June 25, '65.

10

NAMES AND RANK.	AGE.	DATE OF MUSTER.	TERMINATION OF SERVICE, &c.
Blanchard Andrew J.	30	Sept. 28, '61	To Re-enlist Dec. 2, '63.
Blanchard Andrew J.	32	Dec. 3, '63	Missing since May 16, '64.
Grimes William H.	21	Oct. 11, '61	Expiration of service, Oct. 13, '64.
Hutchinson William	29	May 5, '62	" "
Osborn Stephen H.	34	" 14, '62	Order of War Department, June 13, '65.

Company H.

White Caleb B., Sergt.	26	Oct. 26, '61	For Promotion, Nov. 9, '63.
PRIVATE.			
Beckford Eben	37	Aug. 7, '62	Transferred to V. R. C., Feb. 8, '64.

Company I.

Abbott Adolphus	40	Oct. 16, '61	Expiration of service, Oct. 13, '64.

Company K.

Greenough John W. jr., Corp.	25	Dec. 3, '63	Died of wounds at Hampton Va. June 26, '64.
PRIVATES.			
Cassidy James	30	July 19, '62	Disability—March 26, '63.
Clark Albion J.	23	Aug. 9, '62	" May 7, '63.
Edwards George	19	Oct. 15, '61	To Re-enlist, Dec. 2, '63.
Forness William F.	22	May 27, '62	Disability—Sept. 18, '62.
Greenough John W. jr.,	23	Aug. 2, '62	To Re-enlist, Dec. 2, '63.
Heywood George	25	July 30, '62	Disability— " 6, '62.
Kenney Benjamin M.	32	Aug. 7, '62	Transferred to V. R. C., Feb. 29, '64.
Kennison Orrin W.	32	Aug. 7, '62	Disability—July 25, '63.
McCormick Thomas	18	" 31, '62	Expiration of service, Oct. 13, '64.
Quinn James	30	July 19, '62	Disability—Jan. 14, '63.
Roberts Henry L.	28	" 21, '62	Transferred to V. R. C, Feb. 8, '64.

Unassigned Recruits.

Fish Charles W.	32	Feb. 15, '65	Died at Salem, Sept. 30, '65.
Pinckton William	34	July 14, '62	
Rogers Joseph C.	31	" 21, '62	
Trask Joseph E.	18	Jan. 25, '64	Rejected Recruit, Jan. 27, '64.

Twenty-Fourth Regiment Infantry, M.V.—Three Years.

NAMES AND RANK.	AGE.	DATE OF MUSTER.	TERMINATION OF SERVICE, &c.
George G. Wildes, Chap.		July 1, '63	Declined Commission.
Edmund B. Wilson, Chap.		Oct. 21, '63	Resigned, July 6, '64.
George F. Austin, Capt.	23	Sept. 2, '61	" Sept. 1, '62.
John Daland, Capt.	23	"	Expiration of service, Sept. 2, '64.
George W. Gardner, Capt.	27	Aug. 27, '62	" " Oct. 14, '64.
James B. Nichols, Capt.	30	June 27, '63	Disability—Sept. 1, '64.
B. Frank Stoddard, Capt.	31	April 10, '05	Expiration of service, Jan. 20, '66.
George W. Gardner, 1st Lieut.	27	Sept. 2, '61	Capt. Aug. 27, '02.
James B. Nichols, "	30	"	" June 27, '03.
Charles T. Perkins "	31	March 12, '64	Resigned June 10, '64.
B. Frank Stoddard "	31	Oct. 14, '04	Capt. April 10, '65.
Charles T. Perkins, 2d Lieut.	31	Aug. 27, '62	1st Lieut. March 13, '64.
Nichols William C., Musician.	33	Oct. 10, '61	Order of War Department, Aug. 30, '62.
Stanley Abraham J., "	33	"	"

Company B.

Chipman Charles G., 1st Sergt.	21	Sept. 5, '61	For Promotion, Sept. 30, '63.
Kehew Francis A., Sergt.	27	Dec. 19, '63	Deserted, Sept. 21, '65.
Peach George S., "	27	Sept. 12, '61	Disability—April 22, '64.
Plummer Frank, "	25	" 25, "	To Re-enlist, Dec. 18, '03.
Wiley William F. "	24	" 22, "	
Bly Benjamin, Corp.	23	" 25, "	Disability—June 2, '63.
Chase Charles P. Corp.	23	Dec. 19, '63	Expiration of service, Jan. 20, '66.
Friend Alfred, Corp.	31	Oct. 20, '01	Died of wounds July 17, '63.
Greeley Thomas J., Corp.	20	Dec. 19, '63	Expiration of service, Jan. 20, '66.
Luscomb William H., Corp.	20	"	"
Nolan Francis, Corp.	25	"	"
Abbott Charles J., Wagoner.	22	Oct. 17, '61	Expiration of service, Oct. 17, '64.

PRIVATES.

Chase Charles P.	21	Nov. 12, '61	To Re-enlist, Dec. 18, '63.
Chesley Charles H.	18	Sept. 18, '01	"
Chesley Charles H.	20	Dec. 19, '63	Expiration of service, Jan. 20, '66.
Critchet Charles E.	31	Sept. 25, '61	" Sept. 23, '64.
Greeley Thomas J.	18	" 18, "	To Re-enlist, Dec. 18, '63.
Kehew Francis A.	25	Oct. 17, '61	"
Kehew George	21	"	"
Kehew George	23	Dec. 19, '63	Expiration of service, Jan. 20, '66.
Kehew John H.	20	Oct. 17, '01	To Re-enlist, Dec. 18, '03.
Kehew John H.	30	Dec. 19, '63	Deserted, Aug. 17, '65.
Luscomb William H	18	Sept. 10, '61	To Re-enlist, Dec. 18, '63.
McIntyre George	19	" 18, "	Died of wounds, at Newbern, N. C., April 10, '62.
Nolan Francis	23	Nov. 12, '61	To Re-enlist, Dec. 18, '63.
O'Keefe John	30	Sept. 14, '61	Expiration of service, Sept. 14, '64.
Oldson Francis T.	20	Oct. 17, '61	Died of wounds, Sept. 6, '62.
O Neal Thomas	28	Oct. 19, '61	Disability—Aug. 7, 63
Parker George F.	19	Sept. 30, '61	To Re-enlist Dec. 18, '63.
Parker George F.	21	Dec. 19, '63	Disability—July 21, '05.
Reed Thomas	34	Oct. 5, '61	Expiration of service, Oct. 5, '64.

NAMES AND RANK.	AGE.	DATE OF MUSTER.	TERMINATION OF SERVICE, &C.
Scates David M.	26	Oct. 23, '61	Disability—Oct. 28, '62.
Sinclair David	36	" 3 '61	To Re-enlist Dec. 18, '63.
Sinclair David	38	Dec. 19, '63	Expiration of service, Jan. 20, '66.
Willey Albert W.	20	Sept. 25, '61	Disability—Sept. 12, '62.

Company C.

Perkins Charles T., 1st Sergt.	31	Oct. 24, '61	2d Lieut., Aug. 27, '62.
Stoddard Benjamin F., Sergt.	21	" 15, "	To Re-enlist Jan. 3, '64.
Stoddard Benjamin F., "	23	Jan. 4, '64	1st Lieut., Nov. 5, '64.

Company D.

Brown Patrick		Dec. 1, '61	Disability—April 15, '63.
Clark Sylvester		" 5, "	Killed at Little Washington, N. C. Sept. 6, '62.
Ford Charles F.		" 1, "	Disability—April 15, '63.
Mahoney John C.	33	" 3, "	To Re-enlist Jan. 1, '64.
Mahoney John C.	35	Jan. 2, '64	Expiration of service, Jan. 20, '66.

Company E.

Edgerly Samuel A., Sergt.	22	Oct. 15, '61	Expiration of service, Oct. 15, '64.

Company G.

Shaw Walter G. C. C., Corp.	21	Feb. 24, '64	Expiration of service, Jan. 20, '66.
PRIVATES.			
Symonds Henry A.	18	" 18, "	" "
Willey Albert W.	24	" 24, "	" "

Company H.

Coughlin Thos H., Wagoner.	23	Jan. 4, '64	Expiration of service, Jan. 20, '66.
PRIVATES.			
Brown Oliver	41	Oct. 30, '61	" " Oct. 29, '64.
Coughlin Thomas H.	21	" 10, "	To Re-enlist Jan. 3, '64.
Edwards Richard L.	40	July 28, '62	" "

NAMES AND RANK.	AGE.	DATE OF MUSTER.	TERMINATION OF SERVICE, &c.
Edwards Richard L.	42	Jan. 4, '64	Expiration of service, Jan. 20, '65.
McLaughlin Michael	23	Sept. 18, '61	" " Sept. 17, '64.
Mullen Patrick A.	32	Oct. 12, "	Killed at Deep Run, Va., Aug. 14, '64.
Noonan John	21	Nov. 14, '61	Disability—May 13, '64.

Twenty-Sixth Regiment Infantry, M.V.,—Three Years.

Company D.

Davis Benjamin T.	33	Oct. 18, '61	Transferred to 5th U.S. Art., Feb. 7, '63
Warner William W.	23	Sept. 17, "	To Re-enlist Dec. 31, '63.

Twenty-Eighth Regiment Infantry, M.V.—Three Years.

Company A.

Schopic Leo	29	July 21, '64	Deserted, June 12, '65.

Company B.

Bowen Francis	28	July 23, '64	Expiration of service, July 9, '65.

Company C.

Magrath David, Corp.	23	Dec. 13, '61	Transferred to V. R. C., March 15, '64.
PRIVATE.			
Tschopik Leo	21	July 21, '64	

Company D.

NAMES AND RANK.	AGE.	DATE OF MUSTER.	TERMINATION OF SERVICE, &c.
Hackett Michael	32	July 26, '64	Expiration of service, June 30, '65.
Nugent John	34	"	" " " July 5, "

Company E.

Coughlin Edmund C.	18	Dec. 13, '61	Expiration of service, June 29, '65.
Regan Stephen	21	"	Transferred to V. R. C., Feb. 15, '64.

Unassigned Recruits.

Cane Thomas	30	July 19, '64	
Delmer Henry	21	" " "	
Franklin George	36	" 26, "	
Johnson Louis	19	" 23, "	
Kelley James	22	" 19, "	
Matthews Henry	33	" 25, "	
McCormick Thomas	21	" 23, "	
Stevens John	22	" 27, "	

Twenty-Ninth Regiment Infantry, M V.—Three Years

Company B.

Beckett William H.	20	July 21, '64	Expiration of service, July 29, '65.

Company F.

O'Sullivan Timothy	45	Nov. 18, '61	Disability—Oct. 22, '62.

Company H.

Dominick Joseph	21	Dec. 14, '61	Disabilty—May 26, '65.
Galloway John H.	21	"	

Company I.

NAMES AND RANK.	AGE.	DATE OF MUSTER.	TERMINATION OF SERVICE, &c.
Kezar Walter A., Sergt. -	28	Jan. 18, '62	Disability—Sept. 9, '62.
PRIVATES.			
Gardner Benjamin F. -	24	" 14, "	Expiration of service, May 24, '64.
Gove Charles F. -	26	"	May '62.

Unassigned Recruit.

Clark Patrick -	23	Aug. 6, '64	

THIRTIETH REGIMENT INFANTRY, M.V.—THREE YEARS.

Charles A. K. Dimon, 1st Lieut. -	20	Feb. 2, '62	Major 2d Louisiana Vols., Oct. 20, '62.

Company A.

Kelly Thomas, Sergt. -	29	Oct. 3, '61	To Re-enlist Jan. 1, '64.
PRIVATES.			
Garrity John -	32	Sept. 30, '61	To Re-enlist Jan. 1, '64.
Garrity John -	34	Jan. 2, '04	Expiration of service, July 5, '66.
Monarch Eben -	42	Oct. 9, '61	To Re-enlist Jan. 1, '04.
Monarch Eben -	44	Jan. 2, '64	Expiration of service, July 5, '66.
Sherwin William jr. -	19	Oct. 2, '61	" " Oct. 17, '64.
Hassett Martin -	21	Dec. 9, "	Died at Baton Rouge, La., Aug. 9, '63.

Company D.

Kittredge Henry A., Corp. -	44	Oct. 30, '61	Died at New Orleans, La., Aug. 5, '62.
PRIVATES.			
Baker Henry C. -	25	Sept. 15, '62	Assigned from 50th Inf., Jan. 19, '65.
Brown Henry jr., -	33	Nov. 30, '61	To Re-enlist Jan. 1, 64.
Brown Henry jr., -	35	Jan. 2, '04	Disability—July 11, '65.
Kittredge Henry -	43	April 3, '62	Died at New Orleans, La., Oct. 9, '62.
Stevenson Robert -	31	Nov. 30, '61	Jan. 16, '64.

Company E.

NAMES AND RANK.	AGE.	DATE OF MUSTER.	TERMINATION OF SERVICE, &c.
Astrom Carl	21	Dec. 11, '61	Expiration of service, Dec. 22, '64.

Company F.

Hayes Maurice	32	Nov. 13, '61	Died at Baton Rouge, La., Dec. 8, '62.

Company H.

Crowley Philip	40	Jan. 1, '62	Died at Carrolton, La., Aug. 24, '62.

Company I.

Bruce Daniel J.	22	Dec. 28, '61	Promoted to U. S. C. T., June 2, '63.

THIRTY-SECOND REGIMENT INFANTRY, M.V.,—THREE YEARS.

Charles A. Dearborn jr., Capt.	22	Aug. 14, '62	Killed at Fredericksburg, Va., Dec. 13, '62.
Charles A. Dearborn jr., 1st Lieut.	21	Nov. 14, '61	Capt., Aug. 14, '62.
Monaghan Jos., Com. Sergt.	23	March 29, '64	Order of War Department, Aug. 30, '64.

Company A.

Farnum Henry A.	35	Nov. 14, '65	Disability—July 30, '62.
Goodhue Amos D.	18	Aug. 14, '62	Transferred to V. R. C., March 15, '64

Company B.

McFadden Albert	25	July 10, '63	Expiration of service, June 29, '65.
Toomey John	20	Jan. 14, '64	" "

PATRIOTS OF SALEM. 81

Company C.

NAMES AND RANK.	AGE.	DATE OF MUSTER.	TERMINATION OF SERVICE, &c.
Brady Patrick R.	24	Feb. 27, '64	Expiration of service, June 29, '65.
Vaughn Charles E.	18	Nov. 15, '01	To Re-enlist, Jan. 4, '64.

Company D.

Jennis James D.	33	Aug. 14, '62	Disability—March 25, '63.
Jennis Thomas J.	23	" 13, '62	Transferred to V. R. C. July 18, '64.
Powers Edward	20	March 28, '64	Expiration of service, June 29, '65.

Company E.

Fitzpatrick John	23	Nov. 12, '63	Expiration of service, June 29, '65.

Company F.

Phinney Edwin, Corp.	24	Dec. 31, '63	Disability May 27, '65.

Company H.

Roarke Thomas, Musician.	18	Aug. 19, '62	To Re-enlist, Jan. 4, '64.
Roarke Thomas, Musician.	20	Jan. 5, '64	Expiration of service, June 29, '65
PRIVATES.			
Mulhane Martin	25	Aug. 11, '62	Deserted.
Wynder Thomas	26	Sept. 10, '64	Expiration of service, June 29, '65.

Company L.

Schwitzer George	27	Aug. 29, '63	Expiration of service, June 29, '65.
Scheledel Otto	22	" 28, '63	" "

Company M.

Robinson Edward L., 1st Sergt.	25	Sept. 6, '61	Transferred to V. R. C., July 18, '64.

11

NAMES AND RANK.	AGE.	DATE OF MUSTER.	TERMINATION OF SERVICE, &c.
PRIVATES.			
Adams Henry J.	25	July 13, '63	Transferred to V. R C., July 18, '64.
Bonner John	23	Sept. 1, '63	Expiration of service, (absent sick) June 29, '65.
Butman Luther C.	37	July 16, '63	Order of War Department, June 19, '65.
Roark Frank	28	" 6, '64	Expiration of service, June 29, '65.

Unassigned Recruit.

Bolend James	22	Sept. 3, '63.	

THIRTY-FIFTH REGIMENT INFANTRY, M.V.—THREE YEARS.

Samuel C. Oliver, Capt.	32	Aug. 12, '62	Major 2d H. Art., Aug. 27, '63.
Charles F. Williams jr., 2d Lieut.	21	"	Died of wounds, Sept. 22, '62.
Thorndike D. Hodges, 2d Lieut.	26	Jan. 1, '63	Promotion, May 30, '63.

Company F.

Grant Frederick, 1st Sergt.	28	July 19, '62	Nov. 19, '63.

THIRTY-NINTH REGIMENT INFANTRY, M V.—THREE YEARS

Charles L. Peirson, Col.	30	July 13, '64	Disability—Jan. 4, '65 as Lieut. Col.
Charles L. Peirson	28	Aug. 30, '62	Col., July 13, '64.

Company A.

Butlar Benjamin F.	29	Aug. 18, '62	Transferred to Navy, April 21, '64.
Richardson William L.	20	"	Expiration of service, June 2, '65.

PATRIOTS OF SALEM.   83

Company G.

NAMES AND RANK.	AGE.	DATE OF MUSTER.	TERMINATION OF SERVICE, &c.
Andrew A. Chipman, 1st Sergt.	27	June 5, '64	Order of War Department, Aug. 23, '64.

FORTIETH REGIMENT INFANTRY, M. V.—THREE YEARS.

Joseph A. Dalton, Lieut. Col.	-	46	Sept 2, '62	Disability—Jan. 25, '64.
John Pollock, " "	-	25	Feb. 4, '65	Expiration of service, June 16, '65.
Joseph A. Dalton, Major.	-	46	Aug. 20, '62	Lieut. Col., Sept. 2, '62.
A. Parker Browne, "	-	28	" 26. '63	Resigned, March 5, '64.
Charles G. Cox, "	-	26	June 2, '64	Resigned, Dec. 2, '64.
John Pollock, "	-	24	Dec. 7, '64	Lieut Col., Feb. 4, '65.
J. Henry Thayer, Chap.	-		Sept. 17, '62	Resigned, May, 15, '63.
Augustus M. Haskell, Chap.	-	31	" '63	" March 6, '64.
Daniel H. Johnson jr., Capt.	-	27	Aug. 20, '62	" Feb. 25, '63.
Henry F. Danforth, "	-	25	" 23, '62	Disability—Feb. 24, '64.
Richard Skinner jr., "	-	43	Nov. 8, '62	" Jan. 25, '64.
John Pollock, "	-	24	Jan. 26, '64	Major, Dec. 7, '64.
Charles G. Cox, "	-	25	Feb. 25, '64	" June 2, '64.
Charles W. Chase, Capt.	-	21	" 18, '65	Expiration of service, as 1st Lieut. June 16, '65.
Joseph H. Webb, 1st Lieut.	-	31	Aug. 20, '62	Resigned, Dec. 8, '62.
A. Parker Browne, 1st Lieut.	-	27	" 25, '62	Major, Aug. 26, '63.
George C. Bancroft, 1st Lieut.	-	25	Dec. 9, '62	Killed at Old Church, Va., June 1, '64.
John Pollock, 1st Lieut.	-	23	June 27, '63	Capt. Jan. 26, '64.

Company B.

Webb Augustine F., 1st Sergt.	-	21	Aug. 22, '62	2d Lieut., Dec. 9, '63.
Pickett Charles, 1st Sergt.	-		Sept. 3, '62	Expiration of service, June 16, '65.
Grush Benjamin S., Sergt.	-	42	Aug. 22, '62	Expiration of service, June 16, '65.
Nichols James W., Sergt.	-	21	"	2d Lieut., June 2, '63.
Russell John H., "	-	18	"	Expiration of service, June 16, '65.
Call Aaron W., Corp.	-	23	"	" "
Davis Samuel, Corp.	-	30	"	" "
Edwards George W., Corp.	-	23	"	Died at Folly Island, S.C., Sept. 12, '63.
Jewell Charles S., Wagoner.	-	30	"	Transferred to V. R. C., Dec. 15, '63.

PRIVATES.

Anderson George F.	-	18	Aug. 22, '62	Order War Department, May 18, '65.
Ballard Francis A.	-	19	"	Transferred to V. R. C., June 15, '65.
Bissell Wesley T.	-	18	"	Disability—April 10, '64.
Call Isaac	-	18	"	Transferred to V. R. C., Nov. 15, '63.
Kilham Alexander S.	-	20	"	Disability—May 11, '63.
Kimball Joseph A.	-	28	"	Order of War Department, June 30, '65.

NAMES AND RANK.	AGE.	DATE OF MUSTER.	TERMINATION OF SERVICE, &C.
Lahey Jeremiah	37	Aug. 22, '62	Expiration of service, (absent sick) June 16, '65.
Norwood Alexander	43	"	Disability—Sept. 21, '63.
Nutting Joseph H.	18	"	Expiration of service June 16, '65.
Rowe George E.	18	"	" "
Thorner Samuel R.	19	"	Disability—Nov. 18, '62.
Webb Henry jr.	21	"	Order of War Department, June 8, '65.

Company D.

NAMES AND RANK.	AGE.	DATE OF MUSTER.	TERMINATION OF SERVICE, &C.
Wilson Jacob H., 1st Sergt.	26	Sept. 3, '62	2d Lieut., June 9, '63.
Bulger James, Sergt.	20	"	Expiration of service, June 16, '65.
Busted Andrew "	22	"	Transferred to V. R. C., Jan. 10, '65.
Chase Charles W., Sergt.	19	"	1st Lieut., Sept. 7, '64.
Guilford Samuel W., "	28	"	Killed at Cold Harbor, Va., June 3, '64
Pratt Jonathan "	26	"	Expiration of service, June 16, '65.
Cochran James, Corp.	29	"	" "
Gwinn Edward A., Corp.	35	"	Died of wounds, June 27, '64.
Kyle Robert, Corp.	20	"	Killed at Hatchers Run, Va., May 20, '64.
Cunniff Martin, Musician.		"	Principal Mus., May 1, '63.
PRIVATES.			
Dalton Patrick	24	"	Transferred to V. R. C., Nov. 15, '63.
Gardner Charles H.	20	"	Expiration of service, June 16, '65.
Martin Edward	44	"	" "
McFarland Peter	27	"	Died at St. Augustine, Florida, Dec. 20, '63.
Miner Jonathan F.	44	"	Order of War Department, June 16, '65.
Miners John T.	44	Sept. 3, '62	Order of War Department, June 10, '65.
Ogden James	29	"	Disability—Jan. 9, '64.
Peach William jr.	24	"	Order of War Department, June 21, '65.
Simonds William	26	"	Disability—Nov. 2, '62.
Simonds William H.	35	"	Expiration of service, June 16, '65.
Symonds Henry A	18	Feb. 18, '64	Transferred to 24th Inf.
Tolman Stephen W.	35	Sept. 3, '62.	Disability—Nov. 2, '62.
Torr Joseph	28	"	Deserted, Dec. 25, '62.
Welman Timothy A.	40	"	Transferred to V. R. C., Aug. '63.
Wiley William	24	Feb. 24, '64	Order of War Department, June 30, '63.

Company G.

NAMES AND RANK.	AGE.	DATE OF MUSTER.	TERMINATION OF SERVICE, &C.
Cox Charles G.	23	Sept. 18, '62	2d Lieut., Aug. 15, '62.

Company K.

NAMES AND RANK.	AGE.	DATE OF MUSTER.	TERMINATION OF SERVICE, &C.
Shaw Walter G. C. C.	21	Feb. 24, '64.	Transferred to 24th Inf.

PATRIOTS OF SALEM. 85

Unassigned Recruit.

NAMES AND RANK.	AGE.	DATE OF MUSTER.	TERMINATION OF SERVICE, &c.
Nichols James W.	21	Feb. 26, '64	Rejected recruit, May 1, '64.

FIFTY-FOURTH REGIMENT INFANTRY, M.V.,—THREE YEARS.

Lincoln R. Stone, Surg.	30	April 21, '63	Asst. Surg. U. S. Vols. May 11, '64.
Louis F. Emilio, Capt.	18	May 23, '63	May 30, '64.
Charles G. Chipman, Capt.	22	Dec. 16, '64	Expiration of service, Aug. 20, '65.
Louis F. Emilio, 1st Lieut.	18	April 14, '63	Capt. May 22, '63
Charles G. Chipman, 1st Lieut.	22	Jan. 20, '64	Capt. Dec. 16, '64.
Louis F. Emilio, 2d Lieut	18	March 30, '63	1st Lieut., April 14, '63.
Charles G. Chipman, 2d Lieut.	22	May 31, '63	1st Lieut. Jan. 20, '64.

Company A.

Fletcher Francis A., Sergt.	22	March 30, '63	Expiration of service, Aug. 20, '65.

Unassigned Recruits.

Anderson Joseph	18	Jan. 19, '65	Transferred to 55th Inf.
Cassell Charles C.	32	Sept. 2, '04	"
Cassell John M.	42	" 3, "	"
Chase Jacob C.	22	" 1, "	"
Colman George B.	28	" 3, "	"
Fountain William	44	" 1, "	"
Gibbs William	18	" 3, "	"
James John	22	Jan. 11, '65	"
Paine William	38	July 23, '64	"
Sherman William	23	Sept. 3, '64	"
Smith William A.	15	" 1, "	"
Washington John S.	35	" "	May 15, '65.
Wheatland Simeon J.	38	" 2, '64	"
Williams George	30	" 6 '64	"

Fifty-Fifth Regiment Infantry, M.V.—Three Years.

NAMES AND RANK.	AGE.	DATE OF MUSTER.	TERMINATION OF SERVICE, &C.
Edward S. Stimpson, 1st Lieut.	27	June 7, '63	Resigned, June 6, '64.
Edwin R. Hill, 1st Lieut.	36	Sept. 21, '64	Killed in action, Dec. 9, '64.
Edward S. Stimpson, 2d Lieut.	27	May 23, '63	1st Lieut. June 7, '63.

Company A.

Anderson Joseph	18	Jan. 19, '65	Disability—June 16, '65.

Company B.

Helpin James	27	Oct. 29, '64	Died at Charleston, S. C., April 13, '65
James John	32	Jan. 11, '65	Expiration of service, Aug. 29, '65.

Company F.

Cassell Charles C.	32	Sept. 2, '64	Expiration of service, Aug. 29, '65.
Cassell John M.	42	" 3, "	" "
Chase Jacob C.	22	" 1, "	" "
Coleman George B.	28	" 3, "	" "
Fountain James W.	44	" 1, "	" "
Gibbs William	22	Sept. 3, '64	Killed at Honey Hills, S. C., Nov. 30, '64.
Richardson John H.	26	March 28, '65	Disability—May 16, '65.
Sherman William	23	"	Expiration of service, Aug. 29, '65.
Smith William A.	18	" 1, '65	" "
Williams George	30	March 6, '65	" "
Paine William	38	July 23, '63	Disability—July 16, '65.

Unassigned Recruit.

Griffin Benjamin	23	March 28, '65	Expiration of service, May 15, '65.

Fifty-Sixth Regiment Infantry, M.V.,—Three Years.

B. Frank Stoddard, 1st Lieut	22	Aug. 6, '64	Declined 1st Lieut. 24 Inf.

Company C.

NAMES AND RANK.	AGE.	DATE OF MUSTER.	TERMINATION OF SERVICE, &c.
Sweetzer Benjamin F., Sergt.	23	Dec. 28, '63	Transferred to V. R. C., Jan. 28, '65.

Company D.

French Harry B.	38	Dec. 29, '63	Jan. 14, '65.

Company K.

Artemus John	24	Feb. 4, '64	Disability—July 12, '65.
Hogan James	34	Feb. 25, '64	Died of wounds, Wilderness, Va., May 6, '64.
Fitzpatrick John	28	Dec. 28, '64	On Muster Roll, but no other report.

FIFTY-SEVENTH REGIMENT INFANTRY, M.V.,—THREE YEARS.

Charles Saunders, 1st Lieut.		May 1, '64	Declined Commission.
Charles F. Sherman, 2d Lieut.	20,	June 12, '65	Expiration of service, July 30, '65.

Company A.

Gorman John, Corp.	18	Dec. 5, '63	Order of War Department, June 20, '65
PRIVATES.			
Chase John R.	18	Dec. 5, '64	Order of War Department, Aug. 10, '65
Lee William S.	19	" '63	" "

Company B.

Sherman Charles F., 1st Sergt.		29 Jan. 5, '64	2d Lieut., June 12, '65.
PRIVATE.			
Curtis Alonzo	35	Oct. 1, '64	Expiration of service, July, 30, '65.

Company C.

NAMES AND RANK.	AGE.	DATE OF MUSTER.	TERMINATION OF SERVICE, &C.
Sykes Edwin	29	Feb. 18, '64	Deserted, July 1, ,64.

Company D.

Hayes John	44	Feb. 9, '64	Expiration of service, July 30, '65.

Company E.

Luscomb George W., Sergt.	30	March 4, '64	Expiration of service, July 30, '65.
PRIVATES.			
Durgin Thomas	19	Feb. 4, '64.	" "
Murphy William	23	" "	" "
Sweeny Morgan	21	" 9, '64	Order of War Department, June 7, '65

FIFTY-NINTH REGIMENT INFANTRY, M.V.—THREE YEARS

John Hodges jr , Lieut. Col.	22	Feb. 2, '64	Killed, Aug. 3, '64.
Benjamin F. Milward, 1st Lieut.	19	Jan. 25, '64	Disability—Dec. 8, '64.
Benjamin Symonds			1st Lieut., March 28, '65; Disability—July 20, '65.
Nathan A. Frye, 2d Lieut.		Sept. 11, '63	Commission Revoked.

Company A.

Wiley George E., Sergt.	23	Dec. 5, '63	Killed, July 30, '64.
Gorman John, Corp.	18	".	Transferred to 57th Reg., June 1, '65.
PRIVATES.			
Chase John R.	18	"	Transferred to 57th Reg., June 1, '65.
Francis Joseph	42	"	Killed at Spottsylvania, Va., May 12, '64
Lee Robert G.	25	"	
Lee William R.	19	"	Transferred to 57 Inf., June 1, '65.
Ruth John	18	"	
Wright Nathaniel F	35	"	Disability—Nov. 28, '64.

Company B.

NAMES AND RANK.	AGE.	DATE OF MUSTER.	TERMINATION OF SERVICE, &C.
Benson Samuel B. 1st Sergt.	30	Jan. 5, '64	Order of War Department, Co. E. June 2, '65.
Sherman Charles F., 1st Sergt.	29	"	Tansferred to 57 Inf. June 1, '65.
Upton Edward, Sergt.	27	"	Order of War Department, June 19, '65
PRIVATE.			
Curtis Alonzo	35	Oct. 1, '64	Transferred to 57th Inf., June 1, '65.

Company C.

Piper John F., Sergt.	24	July 25, '64	Order of War Department, May 14, '65
Martin George, A. Musician.	18	Jan. 14, '64	Killed at Petersburg, Va., Feb. 27, '65.

Company D.

Butman George A., Musician.	17	Feb. 9, '64	Died at Petersburg, Va., May 29, '64.
PRIVATES.			
Harrington Daniel	18	"	Died of wounds, March 27, '65.
Hayes John	44	"	Transferred to 57th Inf., June 1, '65.
Ruth Edward	18	"	" "

Company E.

Chandler Isaac H., Corp.	21	Feb. 4, '64	Died of wounds, May 12, '64.
PRIVATES.			
Durgin Thomas	19	"	Transferred to 57th Inf., June 1, '65.
McCabe Patrick	38	"	
McDonnell David	18	"	Died at Alexandria, Va., Aug. 25, '64.
Murphy William	23	"	Transferred to 57th Inf., June 1, '65.
Sweeny Morgan	21	"	" "

Company F.

Walker W. A., Sergt.	25	Feb. 20, '64	Disability—June 10, '65.

Company G.

NAMES AND RANK.	AGE.	DATE OF MUSTER.	TERMINATION OF SERVICE, &C.
Luscomb George W., Sergt.	30	March 4, '64	Transferred to 57th Inf., June 1, '65.

Company H.

Oldson Edwin U., Musician.	18	March 12, '64	Disability—Jan. 15, '65.
PRIVATE.			
Roberts George	43	"	Died at Alexandria, Va., Feb. 6, '65.

Company I.

Barrett Peter	41	April 2, '64	Died of wounds, Feb. 16, '65.

Company K.

Preston John F.	22	April 21, '64	Killed at Wilderness, Va., May 6, '64.

SIXTY-FIRST REGIMENT INFANTRY, M.V.,—THREE YEARS.

Company B.

Birmingham John	22	Aug. 25, '65	Discharged, June 4, '65.
Buswell John H.	23	Sept. 12, '64	Disability—June 4, '65.
Hoyt George N.	20	Aug. 29, "	Expiration of service, June 4, '65.
Lundy Michael	44	Sept. 1, "	" "
Small William M.	39	Aug. 31, "	" "

Company D.

Broderick Dennis	33	Sept. 2, '64	Expiration of service, June 4, '65.
Cronin John	33	Aug. 23, "	Disability— " "
Taylor Peter	23	Aug. 25, "	" "

Company E.

NAMES AND RANK.	AGE.	DATE OF MUSTER.	TERMINATION OF SERVICE, &c.
Rowe James H.	27	Sept. 21, '64	Died Nov. 8, '64.

Company I.

Terrance Edward	-	30	Jan. 30, '65	Expiration of service, July 16, '65.

SIXTY-SECOND REGIMENT INFANTRY, M.V.—THREE YEARS

Charles S. Emerson, 2d Lieut.		March 2, '65	Never Mustered.

Company A.

Hall James A.	-	18	March 17, '65	Expiration of service, May 5, 65.
Stevens Samuel	-	29	" " "

Company C.

Gorten Samuel, Sergt.	-	24	March 13, '65	Expiration of service, May 5, '65.
Danforth George, Corp.	-	22	April 13, '65	" "
PRIVATES.			
Barnett Patrick	-	23	" 12, "	" "
French John	-	22	" "	" "
Ivory John	-	21	" 4, "	" "
McAdams Patrick	-	32	" 12, "	" "
McSweegan James	-	23	" "	" "

Company D.

Atkinson Frank E., 1st Sergt.	-	March 27, '65	Expiration of service, May 5, '65.
Atwood Frank, "	-	" "	" "
Conway Dennis, Sergt.	-	" 29, "	" "
Conway James, "	-	" "	" "
Kezar George W., Sergt.	-	March 29, '65	" "

PATRIOTS OF SALEM.

NAMES AND RANK.	AGE.	DATE OF MUSTER.	TERMINATION OF SERVICE, &C.
Sterling William S., Sergt.	-	March 29, '65	Expiration of service, May 5, '65.
Ford Stephen, Corp.	-	" 15,	" "
Noyes George S., "	-	" 23,	" "
Varina William, "	-	" 29,	" "
PRIVATES.			
Berry James A.	-	"	" "
Binney Thomas J.	-	"	" "
Brown Charles W.	-	April 11,	" "
Breed Frank S.	-	" 3,	" "
Cheney Richard R. W.	-	March 4,	" "
Clark John W.	-	April 5,	" "
Conant George W.	-	" 6,	" "
Daley Lewis T.	-	" 3,	" "
Dailey Thomas	-	" 4,	" "
Ferrick James	-	March 21,	" "
Foley James	-	" 29,	" "
Gibbions Lyman O.	-	April 3,	" "
Haley James	-	" 21,	" "
Hilton Charles H.	-	" 4,	" "
Higgins Thomas	-	" 6,	" "
Mauser John B.	-	" 31,	" "
Madden Stephen	-	" 4,	" "
Messenger Hugh G.	-	" 29,	" "
Morse James	-	" 11,	" "
Noyes Charles W.	-	" 4,	" "
Packard William	-	March 27,	" "
Patten Frank	-	" 6,	" "
Sinclair James	-	April 4,	" "
White John	-	"	" "
Wiggins George A.	-	March 6,	" "
Westwood George	-	April 5,	" "
Wentworth Charles F.	-	" 4,	" "

FIRST-COMPANY SHARPSHOOTERS, M.V.—THREE YEARS.

NAMES AND RANK.	AGE.	DATE OF MUSTER.	TERMINATION OF SERVICE, &C.
John Saunders, Capt.	-	Sept. 2, '61	Killed at Antietam, Md., Sept. 17, '62.
George C. Gray, 2d Lieut.	25	"	Resigned May 30, '62.
Stone Charles, Corp.	23	Feb. 16, '64	Order War Department, June 12,' 65.
PRIVATES.			
Adams Charles P.	22	March 17, '62	Disability—Sept. 16, '62.
Gifford Charles P.	19	Nov. 24, '61	Died July 1, '62.
Gray Joseph	39	Sept. 2, '61	Disability—Jan. 27, '63.
Stone Charles	21	"	To Re-enlist Feb. 16, '64.

PATRIOTS OF SALEM. 93

Second Company Sharpshooters, M.V.—Three Years.

NAMES AND RANK.	AGE.	DATE OF MUSTER.	TERMINATION OF SERVICE, &c.
Lewis H. Wentworth, Capt.	39	Sept. 24, '61	Resigned July 16 '62.
Lewis H. Wentworth, Capt.	40	Aug. 20, '62	Disability—May 18, '63.
Robert Smith "	23	May 19, '63	Expiration of service, Oct. 17, '64.
Charles D. Stiles, 1st Lieut.	24	Sept. 24, '61	Resigned Aug, 4, '62.
Edward Upton "	24	Aug. 6, '62	Disability—Jan. 29, '63.
Robert Smith "	22	Jan. 30, '63	Capt. May 19, '63.
Alvan A. Evans, 1st Lieut.	21	Sept. 24, '61	Resigned July 5, '62.
Robert Smith 2d Lieut.	21	July 7, '62	1st Lieut. Jan. 30, '63
Edward Upton, 1st Sergt.	24	Sept. 20, '61	1st Lieut. Aug. 6, '62.
Smith Robert, Sergt.	21	" 16, "	2d Lieut. July 7, '62.
Archer William H., Corp.	40	" 14, "	Disability—Dec. 29, '62.
Batchelder John H. "	43	" 13, "	" Nov. 29, '62.
Thomas Charles S. "	27	" 20, "	" April 15, "

PRIVATES.

Adams Henry J.		25	July 13, '61	Transferred to 32d Inf., Oct. 26, '64.
Archer Benjamin F.		18	Aug. 13, '62	Disability—June 30, '63.
Allen William H.		32	Oct. 3, '61	" Oct. 1, '62
Berg William R.		27	Sept 16, '61	Disability—Jan. 30, '63.
Clements Charles H.		18	Aug. 28, '61	" Sept. 22, '62.
Crane Albert J.			Oct. 5, '61	Discharged Oct. 17, '64.
Clemons William H.		21	Aug. 11, '62	Expiration of service, Oct. 17, '64
Gage Andrew J.		41	Sept. 19, '61	Disability—Oct. 1, '61.
Gardner Abel		24	" 26, "	" Sept. 22, '62.
Grosvenor Edward P.			Oct. 5, "	On Muster Roll, but no other report.
Gardner James W.		35	Aug. 27, '62	Expiration of service, Oct. 17, '64.
Gallnear Charles		45	Dec. 23, '63	Killed at Laurel Hill, Va., May 10, '64
Hutchinson George C.		38	" 26, "	Transferred to V. R. C., March 10, '64.
Knowlton George W.		23	" "	Disability—Dec. 30, '62.
Lewis George B.		26	July 13, '63	May '64.
May Henry E.		44	Aug. 30, '62	Transferred to V. R. C., Sept. 10, '63.
McKenzie John W.		40	July 13, '63	Killed at Spottsylvania, Va, May 10, '64
Meady Daniel F.		34	Sept. 7, '61	Expiration of service, Oct. 17, '64.
Melcher Levi L.		25	Sept. 13, '61	Disability—May 1, '62.
Morrison John		21	Aug. 28, '63	Killed at Spottsylvania, Va., May 10,'64
Miller Allen jr.		19	Sept. 16, '61	Discharged, Oct. 17, '64
Osgood Cyrus M.		28	Sept. 2, '62	Died of wounds at Chancellorsville, Va., May 27, '64.
Roberts Stephen		38	Aug. 30, '62	Expiration of service, Oct. 17, '64.
Roberts John		38	Aug. 30, '62	Discharged, Oct. 17, '64.
Sikey William H.		44	" 11, '62	Expiration of service, Oct. 17, '64.
Stillman Samuel		23	" "	Killed at Laurel Hill, Va., May 8, '64.
Trask Moses A.		39	" 25, "	Expiration of service, Oct. 17, '64.

Veteran Reserve Corps.

Abbott Adolphus		40	Feb. 14, '65	
Arrington James		32	July 7, '64	Order War Department, Nov. 8, '65.

94 PATRIOTS OF SALEM.

NAMES AND RANK.	AGE.	DATE OF MUSTER.	TERMINATION OF SERVICE, &c.
Barnard Samuel	27	July 7, '64	
Bixby Joseph H.	22	Sept. 5, '64	
Cook Jeremiah	37	" 12, "	
Daley James P.	36	Aug. 30, '64	Disability—April 6, '65.
Derby Perley	40	July 25, '64	Order War Department, Nov. 17, '65.
Drahan Nichols	20	" 26, "	
Edwards George K.	28	Aug. 24, '64	
Field Charles	48	Sept. 12, '64	
Fyre Daniel M.	22	Aug. 24, '64	Order of War Department, Nov. 17, '65.
Grieve Thomas	21	July 27, '64	Order of War Department, Jan. 30, '66
Janes William H.	24	Oct. 19, '64	
Jewett John W.	22	July 27, '64	Order War Department, Nov. 21, '65.
Johnson Frederick A.	28	Oct. 10, '64	" " " 14, "
Pierce John	36	Aug. 31, '64	
Pope Benjamin C.	23	Dec. 31, '64	Order War Department, Jan. 8, '66.
Preble John	21	Aug. 2, '64	
Quinn John	25	July 14, '64	
Shortell James	33	Nov. 5, '64	
Smith Daniel F.	34	Sept. 13, '64	
Soper Jeremiah	47	Aug. 13, '64	
Swett Francis F.	43	Dec. 30, '64	
Tarbox David	44	Sept. 3, '64	
Tebbetts Andrew R.	37	" 10, '64	
Thomas Richard H.	23	July 7, '64	
Wentworth John	47	Aug. 8, '64	Order War Department, Nov. 27, '65.

REGULAR ARMY.

Fuller Charles G.	30	March 29, '64	Signal Corps.
Gardner William	30	Sept. 28, '64	Third Artillery.
Rice George	27	" 29, '64	Hospital Steward.
Sassfield Edward	29	Oct. 17, '64	Third Infantry.
Sturtles John	27	Sept. 28, '64	" Artillery.
Sullivan Patrick	26	Oct. 3, '64	" "

U. S. VETERAN VOLS. (HANCOCK'S CORPS.)

Arrington Benjamin E.	27	Feb. 9, '65	Discharged Feb. 9, '66.
Hoar Thomas	33	Jan. 19, '65	

U. S. COLORED TROOPS.

Davis George	37	March 8, '65	Fifth Artillery.
Warren Moses	30	"	"
Willis Lewis	29	"	"

OTHER ENLISTMENTS.

NOTE.—Since the compilation of the list of names contained in this book, the Publishers have been enabled to obtain the following, received too late for insertion in their proper places, and of too much importance to be left out altogether, we consider it proper to insert them under the head of

MISCELLANEOUS.

FIRST REGIMENT HEAVY ARTILLERY, M.V.—THREE YEARS.

Company A.

NAMES AND RANK.	AGE.	DATE OF MUSTER.	TERMINATION OF SERVICE, &c.
Morse Henry	19	July 25, '62	Expiration of service, July 8, '64.

Company C.

Arnold Isaac	31	July 30, '63	Expiration of service, July 8, '64.
Batchelder Walter	22	July 26, '62	Expiration of service, Aug. 30, '64.
Billows James	21	Aug. 6, '62	Mustered out, Aug. 31, '65.
Powers John	20	" 15, '61	Re-enlisted, Jan. 5, ,64.
Tarbox William H.	21	July 23, '61	" "

Company D.

Brown Thomas E.	23	July 1, '62	Wounded, May 19, and discharged July 8, '64.
Campbell John C.	23	July 29, '62	Mustered out, July 31, '65.
Davis Andrew L.	18	" 5, '61	Prisoner, Escaped Feb. 26, '64.
Upton Robert	19	"	Mustered out, July 8, '64.

Company E.

Brown James H.	38	Aug. 5, '62	Mustered out, July 8, '64, (absent sick)

Company F.

NAMES AND RANK.	AGE.	DATE OF MUSTER.	TERMINATION OF SERVICE, &C.
McKown John B.	23	July 22, '61	Prisoner, June 22, '64. Died at Milan Ga., Nov. 18, '64.

Company G.

Clarrage Edward D.	23	Aug. 28, '62	Mustered out, July 8, '64.
Usher Horace D.	20	July 20, '62	" "

Company I.

Palmer George	19	Aug. 6, '62	Mustered out, July 8, '64.

Company L.

Ashbell Wyatt	18	March 14, '62	Transferred to Co. E. Died Sept. 24, '64.

Company M.

Lewis Henry	35	July 13, '62	Mustered out, Sept. 30, '63.
Tyler Jesse	34	" 26, '62	Mustered out, July 8, '64.

SECOND REGIMENT HEAVY ARTILLERY, M V.—THREE YEARS

Company B.

Buxton George F., Q. M., Sergt.	24	July 28, '63	Mustered out, Sept. 5, '65.
Morse George W., Sergt.	25	July 19, '63	Mustered out, Sept. 3, '65.
PRIVATE.			
McClellen George H.	21	Sept. 5, '64	Transferred to 17 Reg. Inf., Jan. 17, '65.

Company D.

NAMES AND RANK.	AGE.	DATE OF MUSTER.	TERMINATION OF SERVICE, &c.
Simmons William	27	Aug. 16, '64	Died at Salem, Feb. 9, '65.
Welch William	42	" 22, '63	Deserted, Jan. 31, '65.

Company I.

NAMES AND RANK.	AGE.	DATE OF MUSTER.	TERMINATION OF SERVICE, &c.
Bailey William	32	Sept. 7, '64	Transferred to 17 Inf., Jan. 7, '65.
Kohane Michael	32	" '63	Order of War Department, July 20, '65

Company K.

NAMES AND RANK.	AGE.	DATE OF MUSTER.	TERMINATION OF SERVICE, &c.
Hamblet Samuel H., Sergt.	19	Dec. 22, '63	For promotion to 2d Lieut., June 19, '64, 5th Mass. Battalion

Company M.

NAMES AND RANK.	AGE.	DATE OF MUSTER.	TERMINATION OF SERVICE, &c.
Cassidy James	33	Dec. 24, '63	Mustered out, Sept. 3, '65.
King Peter	22	"	Disability—Aug. 1, '65.

THIRD REGIMENT HEAVY ARTILLERY, M.V.—THREE YEARS.

Company A.

NAMES AND RANK.	AGE.	DATE OF MUSTER.	TERMINATION OF SERVICE, &c.
Wiley Edwin W.	18	Jan. 10, '63	Mustered out, Sept. 18, '65.

Company C.

NAMES AND RANK.	AGE.	DATE OF MUSTER.	TERMINATION OF SERVICE, &c.
Becker Joseph, Corp.	21	Jan. 4, '64	Mustered out, Sept. 18, '65.
Ronan William H., Corp.	27	Feb. 5, '64	Deserted, Aug. 26, '64.
PRIVATE.			
Murphy John	24	July 30, '63	Mustered out, Sept. 18, '65

Company F.

NAMES AND RANK.	AGE.	DATE OF MUSTER.	TERMINATION OF SERVICE, &C.
Rowell Sidney B.	22	Sept. 16, '63	Promoted to 2d Lieut., Nov. 6, '64. Discharged Aug. 27, '65.

Company G.

Welch William	42	Aug. 8, '64	Deserted.

Company M.

Chamberlin Garland	23	Aug. 29, '64	Transferred to 29th unattached H. Art., Discharged as Sergt., June 16, '65.
Colwell Patrick	26	April 5, '64.	Mustered out Sept. 18, '65.
Nimblett John W.	24	Aug. 29, '64	Transferred to 29th Co. unattached H. Art. Discharged June 16, '65.
Phillips Angels	24	" 26, '64	Mustered out June 17, '65.
Trainer Thomas	23	" 29, '64	Transferred to 29th Co. unattached H. Art. Discharged, June 16, '65.
Twiss Joseph C.	44	"	"

Fourth Regiment Heavy Artillery, M.V.—Three Years.

Company B.

Osborn John B.	21	Aug. 18, '64	Mustered out, June 17, '65.

Company I.

Gray George A.	34	Dec. 9, '64	Mustered out, June 29, '65.
Green George W.	18	"	"
McMurphy James F.	18	12, '64	"

Company L.

Beuls William A.	22	Jan. 11, '65	Mustered out, June 30, '65.
Collier John F.	24	Dec. 29, '64	"
Howard Daniel L.	19	Jan 17, '65	"
Moulton Nathan E.	26	Aug. 22, '64	Mustered out as Corp., June 17, '65.
Pike George N.	20	" 20, '64	"

PATRIOTS OF SALEM.

First Battalion Heavy Artillery.

Company A.

NAMES AND RANK.	AGE.	DATE OF MUSTER.	TERMINATION OF SERVICE, &C.
McLord Alfred	18	Feb. 14, '65	Mustered out, Oct. 20, '65.
Morrison George M.	18	"	" "
Wheelan Samuel B.	24	March 3, '63	" "

Company C.

Clark Charles P	45	April 22, '63	Deserted, Aug. 17.
Morse George	30	Sept. 6, '61	

Fourth Battalion Light Artillery, M.V.—Three Years.

Dailey Patrick	18	Feb. 26, '64	Discharged at N. O., Oct. 4, '65.
Hoyt John A.	30	Jan. 4, '61	Re-enlisted Jan. 13, '64. Discharged Oct. 14, '65.
Lynch Patrick	31	Oct. 26, '64	Transferred to 13th Bat., Jan. 17, '65.
Richardson Alfred	39	Sept. 19, '61	
Smith Benjamin F.	27	Jan. 4, '64	Mustered out Oct. 14, '65.
Tutts John A.	23	Sept. 9, '61	Died at New Orleans.

Fifth Battalion Light Artillery, M.V.—Three Years.

Baur Iquace	29	July 14, '64	Mustered out June 12, '65.
Dunnegan Thomas	21	Aug. 20, '64	" "
Phippen Edward A. jr.	24	Dec. 25, 63	Re-enlisted and Mustered out June 12, '65.

Eighth Battalion Light Artillery, M.V.—Three Years.

Brown George A.	32	May 31, '62	Died Nov. 17, '62, of descase.

Ninth Battalion Light Artillery, M.V.—Three Years.

NAMES AND RANK.	AGE.	DATE OF MUSTER.	TERMINATION OF SERVICE, &C.
Goldthwaite Charles A.	19	Dec. 5, '63	Mustered out June 6, '65.
Kell William	44	" 4, '63	" "

Twelfth Battalion Light Artillery, M.V.—Three Years.

O'Hara Patrick J.		29	Nov. 22, '62	Deserted, Dec. '62.

Fourteenth Battalion Light Artillery, M.V.—Three Years.

Gilman Charles B.	18	Feb. 11, '64	Mustered out June 15, '65.
Gilman Simon F.	23	"	" "

Fifteenth Battalion Light Artillery, M.V.—Three Years.

Smith William	20	Dec. 17, '64	Deserted, Jan. 31, '65.

First Regiment Cavalry, M.V.—Three Years.

Company H.

Hilton Edward W.		Sept. 20, '61	Disability—Sept. 13, '62.
Milton Sylvester S. B.	23	Dec. 26, '63	" Oct. 15, '64.
Quinn John		Sept. 20, '61	" Sept. 13, '62.

Second Regiment Cavalry, M.V.—Three Years.

Company H.

NAMES AND RANK.	AGE.	DATE OF MUSTER.	TERMINATION OF SERVICE, &c.
Donahue Patrick F.		Feb. 4, '64	
Murphy Cornelius	21	Dec. 19, '63	Mustered out July 20, '65.
Withington Francis	36	Feb. 6, '62	Deserted, June 3, '63.

Fourth Regiment Cavalry, M.V.—Three Years.

Company C.

Hill Edwin R.	36	Jan. 6, '64	Promoted to Sergt. Discharged Nov. 27, '64, to accept Com. in 55th Reg. Infantry.

Sixtieth Regiment Infantry,—One Hundred Days.

Company E.

Howes Christopher H.	19	July 23, '64	Expiration of service, Nov. 30, '64.

Second Unattached Company Infantry,—One Hundred Days.

Herrick Benjamin F., 1st Sergt.	33	Dec. 12, '64	Expiration of service, July 7, '65.

Fifth Regiment Infantry,—Nine Months.

Searles George	34	Sept. 16, '62	Expiration of service, July 2, '63.

EIGHTH REGIMENT INFANTRY,—NINE MONTHS.

NAMES AND RANK.	AGE.	DATE OF MUSTER.	TERMINATION OF SERVICE, &C.
Smith James S.	30	Oct. 30, '62	Expiration of service, Aug. 7, '63.

FORTY-SECOND REGIMENT INFANTRY,—NINE MONTHS.

Company H.

Crowley Florance	29	Nov. 4, '62	Deserted, Nov. 24, '62.

FORTY-FOURTH REGIMENT INFANTRY,—NINE MONTHS.

Company H.

Ives George A	22	Sept. 12, '62	Expiration of service, June 18, '63.

FORTY-SEVENTH REGIMENT INFANTRY,—NINE MONTHS.

Company F.

Freeze Noah L.	32	Oct. 20, '62	Deserted Nov. 14, '62.
Gardiner Edward L.	27	" 9, '62	Expiration of service, Sept. 1, '63.

Company K.

Dodge George A.	39	Oct. 31, '62	Disability—Dec. 20, '63.

FIFTIETH REGIMENT INFANTRY,—NINE MONTHS.

Chandler Isaac H.	18	Sept. 30, '62	Expiration of service, Aug. 21, '63.

PATRIOTS OF SALEM.

FIFTY-THIRD REGIMENT INFANTRY,—NINE MONTHS.

NAMES AND RANK.	AGE.	DATE OF MUSTER.	TERMINATION OF SERVICE, &C.
Linehan John	28	Oct. 17, '62	Expiration of service, Sept. 2, '63.

TWENTY-SEVENTH UNATTACHED COMPANY INFANTRY,—ONE YEAR.

Corrigan John	18	Dec. 30, '64	Expiration of service, June 30, '65.

SECOND REGIMENT INFANTRY, M.V.—THREE YEARS.

Company B.

Crosson James F.	22	May 25, '61	To Re-enlist Dec. 30, '63. Expiration of service, July 25, '65.

Company C.

Preston John H., Musician.	19	May 25, '61	Disability—Nov. 10, '63.

SEVENTH REGIMENT INFANTRY, M.V.—THREE YEARS.

Brown John B., Musician.	15	Oct. 22, '62	
PRIVATES.			
Donahoe Patrick F.		"	
Whitman William W.	40	"	

NINTH REGIMENT INFANTRY, M.V.—THREE YEARS.

Company A.

Cochrey Bartholomew	20	June 21, '61	Deserted, June 27, '62.

Company B.

NAMES AND RANK.	AGE.	DATE OF MUSTER.	TERMINATION OF SERVICE, &C.
Brown James	23	June 21, '61	Deserted, Dec. 13, '62.
McCarthy Dennis W.	21	Aug. 7, '62	Expiration of service, June 21, '64.

Company D.

McLaughlin James	20	June 11, '61	Expiration of service, June 21, '64.

Company E.

Devine Michael	30	June 21, '61	Expiration of service, June 21, '64.
Quinlan Thomas	30	Aug. 15, '62	Disability—Dec. 18, '62.

Company F.

Cochlin John	34	Aug. 12, '62	Mustered out, Nov. 1, '63.
Dempsey James	13	June 11, '61	Expiration of service, June 21, '64.
Dinsmore William		"	"
Donelly Patrick O.	21	June 2, '62	Deserted.
Gorman Thomas	18	Aug. 19 62	Transferred to V. R. C., Feb. 6, '64.
Kelly James	24	June 21, '61	Expiration of service, June 21, '64.
Kennelly David	23	Aug. 6, '62	"
McCarthy John	34	June 11, '61	Disability—June 16, '63.
McGrath John	29	"	Discharged at Washington, D. C.
Mahoney Dennis	40	"	Transferred to Navy, as Daniel D.
Murphy Michael	44	Nov. 9, '61	Disability—Oct. 22, '62.
Moynahan Humphrey	24	June 11, '61	Expiration of service, June 21, '64.
McSweeney Morgan	19	Feb. 11, '62	"
McGuire Patrick		June 11, '61	Killed at Battle of Gaines Mill, June 27, '62.
Morrissey John	27	"	Killed at Fredericksburg, Dec. 13, '63.
O'Brien John 1st	24	"	Discharged at Minot's Hill, Va.
O'Keefe John	24	"	Expiration of service, June 21, '64.
Rouke John	22	"	Expiration of service, June 21, '64.
Sortell James	20	"	"
Sweeney Daniel	20	"	"
Shea Patrick	30	"	Died of wounds, May 31, '64.
Shea Timothy		July 31, '62	Expiration of service, June 21, '64.

ELEVENTH REGIMENT INFANTRY, M.V.—THREE YEARS.

Company D.

Crowell Freeman	19	Dec. 14, '61	Expiration of service, Dec. 14, '64.

Company E.

NAMES AND RANK.	AGE.	DATE OF MUSTER.	TERMINATION OF SERVICE, &c.
Millett William S.	19	Jan. 8, '62	Transferred to 11th Battery, and Discharged Jan. 8, '65.

Company F.

Brown John B.	28	Jan. 8, '62	Died at Yorktown, July 8, '62.
Collins John	35	"	Re-enlisted, Discharged July 14, '65.
Nugent Sylvester	44	"	Disability—Aug. 19, '62.
Rogers Joseph S. S.	22	"	Expiration of service, Dec. 14, '64.
Tarbox Randall	19	"	Died at Hannon's Landing, Aug. 15, '62

Company H.

Blanchard Daniel	19	Jan. 27, '62	Discharged, July 14, '65.

Company K.

Allen Benjamin	33	Jan. 8, '62	Died Aug. 30, '64.
Holden John	43	"	Discharged March 4, '63.
Ingalls John	18	"	Died near Falmouth, Va.

TWELFTH REGIMENT INFANTRY, M.V.—THREE YEARS.

Company D.

Grimson Thomas L.	24	July 10, '61	Missing in action, Aug. 30, '62.

Company K.

Driscoll John O.	19	July 10, '61	Discharged on account of wounds, March 5, '63.

Thirteenth Regiment Infantry, M.V.—Three Years.

Company A.

NAMES AND RANK.	AGE.	DATE OF MUSTER.	TERMINATION OF SERVICE, &C.
Dudley L. E.	19	July 27, '61	For promotion, Jan. 3, '63.

Company C.

Lord Henry C.	26	July 27, '61	Dis. on act. of wounds, Nov. 26, '62.

Company E.

Austin Orlow	20	July 29, '61	Expiration of service, Aug. 1, '64.

Company G.

Morton George	30	July 29, '63	Disability—Dec. 14, '63.

Seventeenth Regiment Infantry, M.V.—Three Years.

Company B.

Edwards William P.	23	Nov. 29, '62	Re-enlisted, Dec. 23, '63.
Jones Stephen F.	22	July 22, '61	Dis. on act. of wounds, Feb 7, '63.
McDonough Enos	22	"	Expiration of service, Aug. 3, '64.
Mullaly John E.	22	Dec. 13, '61	1st Lieut., Dec. 19, '61. Capt. May 8, '64. Discharged, July 11, '65.
Therin Charles H.	20	Nov. 28, '62	Expiration of service, Aug. 3, '64.
Thomas James	23	Dec. 3, '62	Died Oct. 13, '64.
Trafton Charles	18		Disability—April 2, '62.
Tyler J. H.	18	July 22, '61	Re-enlisted Jan. 5, '64, Dis. July 11, '65
Wooden William	21	Dec. 2, '63	Disability—April 2, '62.

Company C.

Tracy William	29	Oct. 13, '64	Expiration of service, July 11, '65.

Company D.

NAMES AND RANK.	AGE.	DATE OF MUSTER.	TERMINATION OF SERVICE, &c.
Johnson Charles	21	Feb. 3, '65	Order of War Department, June 9, '65

Company G.

Falon Patrick	22	Sept. 12, '61	Deserted, Nov. 9, '61.

Company I.

McShea John	26	July 22, '61	Deserted, Nov. 9, '61.

NINETEENTH REGIMENT INFANTRY, M.V.—THREE YEARS.

Company E.

Corrigan Daniel	28	Sept. 2, '61	Discharged, June 30, '65.

Company H.

Haskell Benjamin F.	18	Dec. 10, '61	Discharged, Oct. 31, '63.
Maloney Edward	18	"	Re-enlisted Dec. 22, '63. Discharged June 30, '65, in Co. E.
McKennan Francis	19	"	Re-enlisted Dec. 22, '63. Deserted, July 19, '64
Murphy Luke	18	Aug. 20, '61	Killed June 25, '62.
Ross William H.	26	Sept. 16, "	Killed at Spottsylvania, May 10, '64.
Smith John A.	13	June 28, '62	Discharged for Disability, March 23, '63

TWENTIETH REGIMENT INFANTRY, M.V.—THREE YEARS.

Company H.

Hart Timothy	-		Prisoner at Bull Run.

Twenty-First Regiment Infantry, M.V.—Three Years.

NAMES AND RANK.	AGE.	DATE OF MUSTER.	TERMINATION OF SERVICE, &c.
Walcott Alfred F., Capt.		April 26, '63	Expiration of service, Aug. 30, '64.
Walcott Alfred F., 1st Lieut.		Oct. 1, '62	Capt., April 20, '63.
Walcott Alfred F. 2d Lieut.		June 20, '62	1st Lieut., Oct. 1, '62.
Walcott Alfred F. Sergt. Major		Jan. 1, '62	2d " June 20, '62.
Walcott Alfred F.		Aug. 26, '61	Sergt. Major, Jan. 1, '62.

Twenty-Third Regiment Infantry, M.V.—Three Years.

Company A.

Knowlton Samuel.		18 Sept. 27, '61	Expiration of service, Oct. 13, '64.

Company B.

Senter William C.		33 Sept. 20, '61	Expiration of service, Oct. 13, '64.
Smith John		28 Oct. 23, "	Disability—Sept. 6, '62.
Very Edwin, Musician.		32 " 27, "	Order War Department, Aug. 30, '62.

Company D.

Kingsley Frank B.		21 July 31, '62	For Promotion in Wilds Brigade.

Company F.

Thornton John		22 May 19, '62	Expiration of service, Oct. 13, '64.

Twenty-Fourth Regiment Infantry, M.V.—Three Years.

Company E.

Arvedson William L.		28 Oct. 28, '61	Disability—Oct. 5, '62.

PATRIOTS OF SALEM.

Company H.

NAME AND RANK.	AGE	DATE OF MUSTER	REMARKS
Ward Charles G., 2d Lieut.	32	Nov. 22, '61	1st Lieut. Co. 2, ..., Mar ..., 1st lk. V. ... 4
PRIVATE			
McFarland Oren	44	" 2, "	Private. D... ..., 2, 5.

Twenty-Fifth Regiment Infantry, M.V.—Three Years.

Company E.

| Fisher C. J....h | — | 27 N..., 27, ... | ... |

Twenty-Seventh Regiment Infantry, M.V.—Three Years.

Company B.

Dwight Freeman	—	—	19 Oct. 3, '61	
Pierce A...n J.	—	—	28 " 4, "	Discharged March 14, '63.
Pierce W. H.	—	—	21 " 4, "	" June 25, '5.

Twenty-Eighth Regiment Infantry, M.V.—Three Years.

Company E.

| Sisle Robert | — | — | ... |

Twenty-Ninth Regiment Infantry, M.V.—Three Years.

Company I.

| Ma..ry T...as A. | — | — | ... N... ... | ... F... ... |
| Sh..r J...eph A. | — | — | 22 De... ... | ... W... ... Va. June 24, '2. |

THIRTY-SECOND REGIMENT INFANTRY, M.V.—THREE YEARS.

NAMES AND RANK.	AGE.	DATE OF MUSTER.	TERMINATION OF SERVICE, &c.
Carey James	21	May 28, '62	Died Oct. 25, '62.

THIRTY-THIRD REGIMENT INFANTRY, M.V.—THREE YEARS.
Company A.

Brady James	22	July 13, '64	Transferred to 2d Inf. Dis. July 14, '65

THIRTY-FIFTH REGIMENT INFANTRY, M.V.—THREE YEARS.
Company B.

Beckett William	20	July 21, '64	Transferred to 29 Inf., June 29, '65.

THIRTY-NINTH REGIMENT INFANTRY, M.V.—THREE YEARS.
Company H.

Cochrain George	22	Sept. 2, '62	Deserted, Aug. 29, '63.

FORTIETH REGIMENT INFANTRY, M.V.—THREE YEARS.
Company B.

Annis Joseph E.	32	Aug. 20, '62	Disability—Feb. 25, '63.

NAMES OF RESIDENTS OF SALEM WHO ENLISTED IN OTHER PLACES.

David Plummer,—Enlisted in the 10th Maine, and was killed in action at Culpepper Court House, Va., Aug. 13, '62.

James Ricker, Sergt.—Enlisted in the 2d Reg., New Hampshire Vols. and died in Salem of wounds received at the battle of the Wilderness, Va., Aug. 26, '62.

William R. Swasey—Enlisted in the 6th Reg., New Hampshire, Vols. and was killed at the battle of Bull Run, Va., Aug. 29, '62.

John A. Rodwell,—Enlisted in the 6th Reg., New Hampshire Vols. and died at Newport News, Va., Aug. 20. '62, of disease.

Elliott C. Dodge, Sergt.,—Enlisted in the 1st Reg. New York Excelsior Brigade, June 22, '61, and promoted to Lieut.

James Gould,—Enlisted in the 1st Reg., New York Excelsior Brigade, June 20, '61. Found on Muster Roll, but no other reports.

Benjamin F. Sweetser,—Enlisted in the 5th New York Reg. Vols.—Found on Muster Roll, but no other report.

John U. Maxfield,—Enlisted in 1st Maine Heavy Art., Dec. 31, '63, was wounded in left wrist and shoulder, April 8, '64 and Sept 28, '64. Discharged, Sept. 11, '65.

Calvin H. Cleaves,—Enlisted in 9th Maine Inf. Sept. 9, '61 and was discharged Dec. 15, '64.

Jeremiah Collins,—Enlisted in the 30 Maine Inf., Sept. 6, '64 and discharged May 17, '65.

Patrick Clynes,—Enlisted in 1st New York Inf., April 23, '61, was wounded, and discharged, May 23, '63.

Robert Gray—Enlisted in the 2d N. Y. Heavy Art., April 28, '61. Lost the sight of right eye. Discharged, Dec. 15, '62.

Geo. W. Davis,—Enlisted in 3d Maine Infantry, April 30, 1861, was wounded in right shoulder, at Gettysburg, Pa., July 2d, 1863, and discharged June 25, 1864.

Chas. E. Colony,—Enlisted in 31st Maine Infantry, March 21, 1864. Discharged June 5, 1865, and Died Oct. 16, 1872.

Peter Butler,—Enlisted in the 8th New Hampshire Inf., Jan. 4, '62. Lost left arm, April 8, '64. Discharged, July 7, '64.

Charles F. Lendholm—Enlisted in the 99th New York Reg. Inf., May 28, '61, discharged at expiration of service, July 2, '64.

John Day,—Enlisted in the 4th Vermont Inf., Sept. '61, was taken Prisoner, escaped and re-enlisted in the Navy.

Arthur S. Williams,—Enlisted in U. S. Engineer Corps., Sept. 17, '61 and discharged for disability, Aug. 16, '62.

James W. Lyon—Enlisted in the 1st R. I. Reg. Inf., May 18, and discharged at expiration of service, Aug. 25, '65.

James L. Phillips,—Enlisted in the 30th Reg. Inf. M. V. Oct. 7, '61 and transferred to V. R. C. Discharged Oct. 10, 64 at N. Orleans, La.

Henry H. Francis,—Enlisted in 3rd Maryland, Reg. Calvary, Sept. 4, '63. Discharged at expiration of service, Sept. 7. '65.

William H. H. Thomas,—Enlisted in 3d Reg. Heavy Art. Oct. 20, '63 and discharged at expiration of service, Sept. 18, '65.

Charles A. Place,—Enlisted in the 12th Reg., N. H. Inf.—Co. A., Aug. 30, '62, and was mustered out at Richmond, Va., July 23, '65.

Andrew J. Thompson,—Surgeon 8th N. H. Vols. Mustered in at New Orleans, La., Aug. 1862. Mustered out at Natchez, Miss., Nov. 1865. 1864 and '65 was Post Surgeon, Post of Natchez and President of Board of Health. 1865 was Surgeon in Chief, District of Natchez, Department of Miss.

RECORD OF SEAMEN AND OFFICERS IN THE NAVAL SERVICE.

NAMES.	AGE.	ENTERED SERVICE.	NAME OF VESSEL, &c.
Adams George W.	-		
Ames Eben	-		
Anderson William	-		
Arvedson C. K.	-		
Avery Henry	-	July 17, '62	—Acting Ensign.
Babson Edwin	-		" "
Bager Henry	21	March 3, '62	2 years—Ship Wachusett.
Bagley Daniel I.	19	April 24, '62	3 " —Hampton Roads.
Baines Richard	25	" 15, '62	3 " —Discharged, June 7, '62.
Barnum S. G.	34	" 24, '62	3 " —W. Flotilla.
Barrett Cornelius	22	March 8, '62	3 " — " "
Barrows Henry	28	May 16, '62	3 " —Rhode Island.
Barry Edward	32	" 6, '62	3 " —Tioga.
Bartlett Jeremiah I.	21	" 17, '62	3 " —Landel's Squadron.
Bassett Eben	30	Feb. 17, "	2 " —Wachusett.
Baxter John	29	March 14, '62	3 " —Sebago.
Beckett Edward	-		
Bell James	38	May 5. '62	3 " —Farragut's Squadron.
Berrin Lewis	23	March 12, '62	2 " —W Flotilla.
Black William	20	May 8, '62	3 " —Farragut's Squadron.
Borden Thomas	-		
Boyd George	32	April 21, '62	3 " —Mahaska.
Bowyer Charles	-		
Bowen James W.	25	April 8, '62	3 years—W. Flotilla.
Bradford Francis	21	Sept. 4, '62	1 "
Bradley James	26	June 4, '63.	2 "
Barrington A.	-		
Braman John	22	May 5, '62	3 " —Tioga.
Brady Thomas	22	Feb. 10, '62	2 " —Constitution.
Bray Isaac	22	" 17, "	2 " —Constitution.
Brown August		July 22, '64	
Brown Charles	24	April 2, '62	2 " —W. Flotilla.
Brown Charles	17	" 19, '62	3 " —Dupont's Squadron.
Brown Edmund A.		Aug. 30, '64	1 " —Brookline.
Brown Herbert A.		May 20, '62	3 " —Housatonic.
Boden Hiram C.	29	Aug. 28, '61	3 "
Brown James	19	Feb. 11, '62	2 " —Western Flotilla.
Brown James R.		Sept. 2, '64	1 " —Rhode Island.
Brown John H.	22	Feb. 18, 62	2 " —San Jacinto.
Bruce Sullivan	38	March 18, '62	—Maritanzic.
Buckley Timothy	22	May 1, '62	—Farragut's Squadron.
Bumpus Elisha		March 19, '62	2 " —W. Flotilla.
Buton Maurice	21	May 13, '62	3 " —Rhode Island.
Carcy George A.	38	July 22, '62	3 " —Farragut's Squadron.
Casey Thomas	18	" 8, '62	3 " —Canandagua.
Cate Samuel A.	25	Aug. 30, '64	1 "
Chandler George A.	22	May 23, '63	1 "
Chase George	20	March 28, '63	1 "
Chapman George T.	-		—Acting Ensign.
Childs C. N.	-		
Clark William	23	Oct. 14, '62	1 " —Colorado.
Clark Patrick	-		
Clarrage James O.	27	May 2, '64	2 " —Circassian.
Cunningham John		Aug. 30, '64	1 " —Ohio, Orvitta, & N. Carolina.

PATRIOTS OF SALEM.

NAMES.	AGE.	ENTERED SERVICE.		NAME OF VESSEL, &c.
Cook Frank				
Darcy Michael		July 26, '64		
Dearborn Henry F.		June 8, '63	1 year —	
Deland Charles	45	March 29, '62	2 years—	
Dix Charles E.	17	April 23, '64	2 "	—Hampton Roads.
Dodd James	22	Aug. 25, '62	1 year	—Philadelphia.
Dodge Judson F.	25	July 15, '63	1 "	
Douglas Albert	22	" 5, '64	2 years—Sabine.	
Dupar William G.		Oct. 20, '64	3 "	
Delmer Henry				
John Day	32	Sept., '63		—Minnesota.
Edwards Shuball				—Acting Ensign.
Evans George				
Finney George				—Acting Master.
Finngan Thomas	28	May 14, '62	3 "	—Housatonic.
Fitzgerald George	22	"	3 "	—Lardner's Squadron.
Fitzgerald William				
Flannigan Thomas	24	Jan. 21, '62	2 "	—Marblehead.
Flemming Hugh	21	May 2, '62	3 "	—Farragut's Squadron.
Flemming Michael	25	" 14, '62	3 "	—Dupont's Squadron.
Fogg James W.				
Ford L. A.				
Fowler Edward	23	July 7, '62	3 "	—Canandagua.
Fowler William W.	19	May 3, '62	3 "	—Mahaska.
Foye Edward				
Francis Moses F.	17	May 3, '62	3 "	—Farragut's Squadron.
Friend Frederick	22	July 22, '64	1 year	—Hawes and Moon.
Furtony Michael	21	May 22, '62	3 years—Dupont's Squadron.	
Gallagher Joseph	22	Aug. 28, '63		
Galloway F. N.		Feb. 10, '65		
Gardner George A.	33	July 18, '63	1 year	
Gass William H.	22	May 12, '62	2 years	
Glass George	28	Aug. 16, "	1 year	—Philadelphia.
Grady Dennis		Aug. 29, '64	3 years—	
Graser Charles	24	July 13, '64		
Green George	28	Jan. 1, '63	1 year—	
Green John				
Grover John C.	16	Oct. 2, '61	2 years—North Carolina.	
Hancock John		" 17, '63		—Midshipman.
Hanshaw John	28	June 27, '64	3 "	
Harmon M. D.	40	April 8, '62	3 "	—Mahaska.
Harrington Daniel	50	Aug. 17, '63		—Midshipman Ohio.
Harrington F. H. W.	32	April 25, '62	3 "	—Hampton Roads.
Hatch Charles F.		July 28, '63		—Master's Mate.
Hawes James	21	" 7, '62	2 "	—Albatross.
Hawthorne William H.		Nov. 9, '63		—Master's Mate.
Hayden Thomas	19	April 5, '62	3 "	—Western Flotilla.
Hayes James				
Hayes Thomas	18	Feb. 13, '62	3 "	—San Jacinto.
Hazard John	30	July 29, '64	1 year	—Harvest Moon.
Higginbottom John		" 14, "		
Hill Thomas	28	Sept. 1, '62	1 "	—Rhode Island.
Hill Thomas G.		April 5, "	3 years	
Holland Thomas	20	July 7, '64	3 "	—Potomac.
Hobbs Nathan F.				
Howard Austin		March 31, '62	3 "	—Western Flotilla.
Hemmenway Frederick	23	April 19, "	3 "	—Hampton Roads.
Hennessy Arthur	23	" 25, "	3 "	—Hampton Roads.
Holmes Francis W.		" 21, "	3 "	—Hampton Roads.
Hood Osborn	15	" 25, "	3 "	
Hughes James				
Hunter John	28	" 7, "	3 "	—Hampton Roads.

PATRIOTS OF SALEM.

NAMES.	AGE.	ENTERED SERVICE.	NAME OF VESSEL, &C.
Humphrey Pendar		Aug. 30, '64	1 year —
Hurd George S.		April 25, '64	
Hurley James	24	" 28, '62	3 years—Hampton Roads.
Hurley John			
Hurty James	21	" 14, "	3 " —Western Flotilla.
Hutchinson Goodwin	18	Feb. 13, "	3 " —Western Flotilla.
Johnson Lewis			
Jackson James W. C.		April 23, "	3 " —Hampton Roads.
James Henry	31	May 31, "	3 " —Engineer Gennessee.
James John		Sept. 3, "	1 year
Jewell David N.	32	April 21, "	3 years—Hampton Roads.
Johnson Peter	22	" 25, "	3 " —Hampton Roads.
Johnson Samuel	24	" 11, "	3 " —Hampton Roads.
Johnson Samuel F.	21	May 8, "	3 " —Lardner's Squadron.
Jones John		July 28, '64	
Jones John J.	26	April 8, '62	3 " —Hampton Roads.
Jones Thomas T.	35	June 4, "	3 " —South Carolina.
Kimball William L.	30		—Princetown.
Kane Dennis F.	18	June 4, '63	1 year —Ethan Allen.
Knight Charles		Sept. 1, '64	—Colorado.
Kavanaugh James		May 29, '63	
Kelly Luke	20	"	
Kelly Charles	24	Feb. 14, '62	3 years—Constitution.
Kelly James	22	June 10, '63	1 year
Kelly Patrick	22	" 27, "	1 "
Kelliher Jeremiah	18	Nov. 11, '62	1 "
Kelliher Mortmon	23	Feb. 8, "	—Wachusett.
Kennedy Martin	38	" 7, "	3 years—Maritanza.
Kennedy Michael	27	" 12, "	3 " —San Jacinto.
Kenney Thomas F.	18	June 5, '63	1 year —Ethan Allen.
Kimball Horace W.	18	" 23, "	1 " —Aries.
King George	22	Feb. 11, '62	3 years—Maritanza.
King Obey	25	" 15, "	3 " —Fireman Constitution.
Kirwin Charles		Sept. 1, '64	2 "
Kirwin Charles	19	May 23, '63	1 year
Kleever Ferdinand	22	Feb. 17, '62	3 years—Constitution.
Knight Solomon	18	June 5, '63	1 year —Ethan Allen.
Knowles David L.	21	May 23, '63	1 "
Knowlton Marcus A.		Sept. 2, '64	1 " —Rhode Island.
Lacey James	19	July 2, '63	1 " —Shenandoah.
Lacey Thomas		"	1 "
Laduc Joseph	28	June 11, '63	1 "
Lancey Patrick	21	" 12, "	1 "
Landgren George O.	18	July 9, '62	3 years—Canandagua.
Landgren John H.	22	"	3 " —Canandagua.
Lawrence John	27	Feb. 10, '62	3 " —San Jacinto.
Leach Robert	53	" 13, "	3 " —Western Flotilla.
Lechood John	22	June 10 '63	1 year.—
Learey Henry	23	" 4, "	1 " —Ethan Allen.
Lee William H.	26	June 15, '64	1 " —Vincennes.
Lee York M.	21	Jan. 3, '62	3 years—Vermont.
Lenakin William	29	June 20, '63	1 year —Eathan Allen.
Lewis Eneas I.	28	Feb. 12, '62	3 years—Marblehead.
Lewis Henry	38	Oct. 27, '63	1 year—
Lewis John		May 28, '63	1 " —Ethan Allen.
Libby Melvin J.	21	June 27, '63	1 " —Aries.
Liles Jack	33	July 2, '63	1 " —Shenandoah.
Little Thomas	33	June 1, '63	1 "
Lobdell Richard T.	30	June 15, '63	1 "
Long Andrew	35	June 9, '63	1 "
Long Henry	26	"	1 "
Loratta Anthony	40	Feb. 10, '62	3 years—San Jacinto.

PATRIOTS OF SALEM.

NAMES.	AGE.	ENTERED SERVICE.		NAME OF VESSEL, &c.
Lowd William H.	18	June 9, '63	1 year	—Ethan Allen.
Lowry Michael	24	" 12, '63	1 "	
Lucey Daniel	23	May 30, '63		—Iron Age.
Luscomb H. R.				
Luscomb Joseph M.		April 24, ,63		—Acting Ensign.
Lynch Charles	23	June 2, '63	1 "	—Ethan Allen.
Lynch Francis E.	24	" 19, '63	1 "	—Aries.
Lynch James	24	July 2, '63	1 "	—Shenandoah.
Lynch John		" 2, '64		
Maddicutt John	19	Jan 18, '64	1 "	—Sacramento.
Malowe John	23	June 18, '64	1 "	—Cornubia.
McCormick Charles		Aug. 5, '64		
McDuffie Dana H.	18	Jan. 19, '64	1 "	
McDuffie George	26	Aug. 18, '62	1 "	
McKinley Barney	18	Jan. 16, '64	1 "	
McLaughlin Andrew	23	" 18, '64	1 "	—Harvest Moon.
McVey Charles	33	"	1 "	—Don and Ohio.
Matthews Henry				
Mehan John C.		Jan, 19, '64		
Miller Fred L.				—Engineer Kearsage.
Miller Thomas	22	Jan. 18, '64	1 "	—Sacramento.
Millett Charles		June 19. 63		—Acting Ensign.
Millett Frank		Aug 5, '63		—Acting Master's Mate.
Morgan Joseph				—Minnesota.
Moran Matthew				
Munroe Robert	17	July 21, '62	3 years	—Farragut's Squadron.
Morgan John A.	40	May 24, '61		—Colorado.
Morgan Joshua	18	May 2, '64		
Murphy Patrick	30	Jan. 18, '64	1 year	
Neal William W.				
Neilson William		Jan. 30, '63		—A. A. Surgeon.
Nichols Arra	21	" 20, '64	1 "	—Sacramento.
Nicholas Benjamin	19	Jan. 29, '64		—Osceola.
Niles Amos		Oct. 28, '64	2 years	
Nutting William G.		Aug. 26, '61		—Acting Lieutenant.
O'Donnell John				
Oldson Charles		May 4, '64		—Mississippi.
Oldson John H.	17	Aug. 17, '62	1 year	—Memphis.
Oldson George D.		" '61	1 "	—Anderson.
Osborne John B.	23	July 15, '63	1 "	
Parker Alfred	28	Jan. 30, '64	1 "	—Massasoit.
Pepper Walter A.	28	April 24, '61	1 "	—Massachusetts. Discharged March 12, '62.
Pepper Walter A.	29	May 2, '62	1 year	—Tioga. Discharged June 14, '64.
Perkins Asa B.	21	July 15, '63	1 year —	
Perry Henry E.	19	May 27, '63	1 "	—
Pierce Thomas	28	Jan. 15, '64	1 "	—Harvest Moon.
Pierce Charles H.		April 9, '62		—Master's Mate. Pro. to Acting Ensign, '63. Sonoma, Santiago de Cuba. Discharged Feb. '65.
Pirt Isaac	30	Jan. 19, '64	1 "	—Sacramento.
Pitman John H.		Oct. 4, '64	1 "	—Acting Master's Mate.
Pope Thomas				
Pousland Edward A.		Feb. 10, '63	1 "	—
Powers Charles H.	22	Oct. 21, '61	2 years	—North Carolina.
Pratt Edward L.	12	Feb. 12, '62	3 "	—Katahdin.
Pratt William A.	21	April 15, '64	1 year	—Canonicus.
Putnam Perley	19	Oct. 24, '61	2 years	—North Carolina.
Rinks John H.	22	May 2, '62	2 "	—Tioga.
Rogers John E.	18	Feb. 11, '62	2 "	—Western Flotilla.
Rollins James	17	Dec 16, '62	3 "	—Philadelphia.

NAMES.	AGE.	ENTERED SERVICE.	NAME OF VESSEL, &c.
Ruth Edward	17	June 24, '62	2 years—Ino.
Selton Thomas E.			
Servey William T.	29	July 14, '63	1 year —Acting Ensign
Shaw John	26	March 10, '64	1 " —Osceola.
Shehan Patrick	22	" 25, '63	1 " —
Sherman William	21	Sept. 6, '62	1 " —
Simpson John A.	40	April 8, '62	1 " —Western Flotilla.
Sluman William H.	42	Feb. 3, '65	2 years—
Smith Albert P.			—Acting Ensign.
Smith Charles	18	Oct. 30, '64	1 year—
Smith Samuel		July 18, '63	—Acting Ensign.
Stevens John			—
Spaulding J. C.			—
Spofford John B.			—
Staples E. C.			—
Stearns William	25	April 4, '63	3 years—Western Flotilla.
Stevenson J. H.			3 " —
Stickney David	29	July 6, '64	3 " —
Sullivan John		" 28, '64	3 " —
Swasey Thomas S. B.	18	Aug. 19, '63	1 year —Ino.
Swasey William M.		July 22, '63	—Acting Ensign.
Tato Charles			—
Thomas Samuel W.	21	May 4, '64	—
Tiviss John W.			—
Waldron James	22	Dec. 30, '64	1 " —Princeton.
Watts Charles	43	Jan. 12, '64	1 " —Sacramento.
Watts Thomas	34	Dec. 17, '64	1 " —Niphone.
Webb James H.			1 "
Webber Joseph	18	Aug. 8, '61	—Surg. Steward.
Weir George C.	22	Jan. 13, '64	1 "
Welch James H.	18	" 4, '64	1 " —
Welch John A.			—Minnesota.
Weston Richmond	20	Dec. 21, '64	1 " —Pequot.
Whalley Thomas	39	" 10, '63	1 " —Sacramento.
Wentworth Ezra N.	19	"	1 " —
Whelan John	26	Jan. 12, '64	1 " —Sacramento.
Whitmarsh Leander	19	" 28, '64	1 " —Osceola.
Whittemore Henry	22	Dec. 19, '64	1 " —
Willey George M.	20	July 15, '63	2 years—Sassacus.
Willey Mark L.	45	Sept. 15, '63	2 " —Sassacus.
Willey Mark L. jr.	18	July 15, '63	3 years—Sassacus.
Willey Edward A.	24	Jan. 29, '64	1 year —
Wilber Wesley	20	" 19, '64	1 " —Sacramento.
Willett Allen	24	" 27, '64	1 " —Osceola.
Williams Edward	29	Dec. 28, '64	1 " —
Williams John	32	July 11, '64	3 years—
Williams John	18	Jan. 22, '64	1 year —
Williams John F.	22	Dec. 4, '64	1 " —
Williams Richard	34	Aug. 17, '64	2 years—John Adams.
Williams Thomas	20	Dec. 19, '64	1 year —
Willis John	31	Jan 18, '64	1 " —
Wilson James	20	Jan. 14, '64	" —Sacramento.
Wilson John H.	27	" 28, '64	1 " —
Wilson Joseph H.	30	July 19, '64	—Ossipee.
Wood Samuel A.			—
Woodbine Abel	36	Dec. 3, '63	1 " Canonicus.
Woodell Eli	25	Jan. 18, '63	1 " —
Wright James	19	" 23, '63	1 " —
Wright Richard	25	" 18, '63	—Sacramento.

LIST OF WOUNDED, COMPILED FROM THE BEST SOURCES.

Adams Charles—Wounded in left hip, Aug., '64.
Aldrich M. H.—Wounded in left leg, June 29, '64.
Arnold Isaac—Wounded in action, May 19, '64.
Arrington James—Wounded on transport off Hatteras.
Bray Parker—Lost right leg.—Oct. 2, '64.
Brown Ezra L.—Wounded in right shoulder June 3, '64, and left leg, March 14, '62.
Ballard George R.—Wounded in left hand and side, June 16, '64.
Burns Charles E.—Lost left leg, Aug. 30, '62.
Busted Andrew—Wounded in right side, June 1, '64.
Browning George F. 1st Lieut.,—Wounded severely at Cedar Mountain, Va., Aug. 19, '62. March 13, '66 was promoted to Capt. and Major by brevet.
Beckett Daniel C.—Wounded in action, May 19, '64.
Barenson A. Frank—Wounded in right side, July 18, '64.
Bickford John M.,—Wounded in action, June 16, '64.
Bradley John,—Wounded in action, May 19, '64.
Brown James 2d,—Wounded and sick at expiration of service, July 8, '64.
Brown Samuel,—Wounded in action, June 16, '64.
Bruce Robert P.,—Wounded severely in right hip, at Spottsylvania Court House, May 19, '64
Bowen Thomas E.,—Wounded severely in right hip, May 19, '64
Bovey James G.,—Wounded severely at Petersburg, Va., June 14, '64.
Ballazar Castano,—Drowned at sea, April 10, '73.
Coggswell William, Lieut. Col.,—Wounded at Chancellorsville, May 3d, '63. Promoted to Col., June 6, and Brigadier General by brevet, Dec. 17, '64.
Cusick Patrick.—Shot through both legs and left for dead on the battlefield at Gaines Mill, Va. Taken by the Rebels and imprisoned at Richmond. Released, July 27, '62.
Cashion Robert,—Wounded in left hand, May 5, '65.
Colony M. G.,—Lost right leg, Sept. 30, '64.
Chipman James G.,—Wounded in action, May 19, '64.
Collier Charles D.,—Wounded in action, June 4, '64.
Colcord David B.,—Wounded at Petersburg, June 22, '64.
Cohane John,—Wounded in hip and shoulder, July 2, '63 and in the wrist, May 5, '64.
Donovan Patrick,—Wounded in the hand, April 9, '63.
Deland Alfred,—Wounded in action, May 19, '64.
Desmond John,—Wounded and discharged, May 2, '63.
Devereux Charles U., Capt.—Wounded severely at the battle of Glendale, June 30, '62.
Darcy Thomas,—Wounded in leg at Gaines Mill, June 27, '62.
De-Boa John,—Wounded in right foot, Va. Died, Sept. 7, '75.
Evans William,—Wounded before Port Hudson, served out his term and was discharged Aug. 24, '63.
Ford Charles T.,—Wounded in left side.
Falow Thomas R.,—Wounded in left leg and left hand, May 8, '64, also in right leg, and right arm June 27, '62.
Frye Daniel M.—Wounded in left arm, Sept. 17, '62.
Fallon Thomas,—Wounded at Gaines Mill, also at battle of Malvern Hill.
Fairfield Samuel G.—Wounded in action, May 19, '64.
Fillebrown Charles F.—Wounded in action, June 16, '64.
Flowers William H. jr.—Wounded in action, May 19, '64.
Ferguson Samuel A.—Wounded in action, June 1, '64.
Ferguson George P.—Wounded in left hand, May 19, '64.
Greenough Daniel S.—Wounded dangerously near Resaca, Ga., May 15, '64, died of the wounds, June 6, '64.
Geegle Edward—Wounded at battle of Malvern Hill, July 1, '62.
Gardner Horace B.—Wounded near Petersburg, Va., June 18, '64, discharged for disability, same year.
Goldthwaite Luther M.—Wounded in leg, May 19, '64.
Goldsmith William H.—Lost left leg, June 7, '64.
Gardner Charles H.—Wounded in right side and knee, June 1, '64.
Getchell Stephen O.—Wounded in action, May 19, '64.
Hale Henry Appleton, 1st Lieut.—Promoted to Asst. Adjutant General of Vols., with rank of Capt. Was wounded severely in the face at Antietam, Sept. 17, '62, and in the instep, at Cold Harbor, June 31, '64.

Hopkins John—Wounded in action, May 19, '64.
Howard Eben N.—Wounded in action, May 19, '64.
Hall Edward A.—Wounded in left shoulder, Dec. 16, '62.
Hitchings A. F.—Wounded in right leg, Dec. 13, '62.
Hobbs George—Lost right arm, Oct. 2, '64.
Jones William—Wounded in left leg, June 30, '64.
Kalher Jeremiah—Wounded in left shoulder, June 18, 64.
Ketcham Francis H.—Wounded in belly, June 23, '64.
Kezar Walter A.—Wounded in action at Oak Swamp, taken prisoner June 29, '62.
Langmaid George W.—Wounded at Chancellorsville, May 3, '63.
Lewellen Thomas J.—Wounded at battle of Wilderness, May 5, '64.
Luscomb William F.—Wounded in Action, May 19, '64.
Lane William H.—Wounded in left ankle and left knee, April 26, and July, '62.
Milton B. S. S.—Wounded.
McCligett James—Wounded in leg, May 16, '64
McCarty John—Lost left leg, at Malvern Hill, July 1, '62.
McLaughlin James—Wounded at Hanover Court House, Va.
Martin Edward—Wounded at Hatcher's Run, Va., May 20, '64.
McGordes Charles—Wounded.
Mellow Henry—Wounded in head, Oct. 19, '64.
Neil Edward—Wounded at Malvern Hill.
Nichols Benjamin C.—Wounded June 19, '64.
Osborn Josiah P.—Wounded in right hip, April 24, '62.
O'Sullivan Timothy—Wounded and taken prisoner at White Oak Swamp, June 29, '62.
O'Hara Patrick—Lost sight of left eye, March, '64.
Patten James N.—Wounded at 1st battle of Bull Run.
Phalen Edward A., Capt.—Wounded severely at Cedar Mountain, Aug. 9, '62.
Preston John H.—Wounded at Darnstown, Md., Oct. 30, '61.
Peach William jr.—Wounded at 10 miles Station, Fla.
Powell Nathaniel—Wounded by splinter, March 8, '62.
Phippen Robert A.—Wounded in action May 19, '64.
Phippen Robert C.—Wounded in action, June 22, '64.
Phipps Henry B.—Wounded in action, May 19, '64.
Pitman Nathaniel F.—Wounded in leg, May 19, '64, at the battle of the Wilderness, the leg
    was amputated and he died June 14, at Mount Pleasant Hospital, Washington, D.C.
Peabody William M.—Wounded in left side, Aug. 5, '62.
Pratt James F.—Wounded in action, June 16, '64.
Porter William F.—Wounded in wrist, May 19, '64.
Purbeck John H.—Wounded in wrist, May 19, '64.
Roach Michael—Wounded in leg, Feb. 11 and June 8, '62.
Rodigrass John S.—Wounded in foot, June 24, '62.
Rice William H. C.—Wounded severely at Winchester, Va., May 25, '62.
Reynolds John P., Capt.—Wounded twice severely at Antietam, Sept. 17, '62.
Ruth John—Wounded May 30, '65.
Randall Charles W.—Wounded in action, June 14, '64.
Reeves Edward—Wounded in action, May 19, '64.
Regan B. F.—Wounded in right hand, May 5, '64.
Sargent Thomas J.—Wounded in left side, May 19, '64.
Sweeney David—Wounded at James Mill.
Smith Samuel H.—Wounded and discharged on that account, Dec. 1, '62.
Shehan Timothy—Wounded in action, May 19, '64.
Solen Nathaniel—Wounded in action, May 19, '64.
Smeathers Joseph—Lost left hand, June 26, '64.
Tobey William—Wounded in left hand, Nov. 27, '63.
Tierney Patrick—Wounded at Malvern Hill.
Tucker Henry G.—Wounded in action, June 22, '64.
Tibbetts George F.—Wounded in action, June 18, '64.
White Caleb B.—Wounded in action at White Hall, N. C.
Walton Edward A.—Wounded in action, May 19, '64.
Warner Clarence A.—Wounded in action, May 19, '64.
Wentworth John H., Sergt.—Wounded in the head, May 19, '64.
Whalan Michael—Wounded in left side and wrist.
Walker William—Wounded while marching into Yorktown, Va.
Wettey Martin—Wounded in the hip, Sept. 17, '62.

PATRIOTS OF SALEM. 119

PRISONERS OF WAR.

First Heavy Artillery, M.V.—Three Years.

James G. Bovey,—1st Sergt. of Co. G. Enlisted Aug. 5, '62 and re-enlisted Dec. 30, '63; and was captured at Petersburg, Va., June 22, '64; and confined in the Libby, Belle Isle, Florence and Charleston Prisons; released from the latter Dec. 16, '64, and discharged, July 31, '65.

George S. Farmer,—1st Sergt. of Co. H. Enlisted July 5, '61; re-enlisted Jan. 2, '64; was captured at Petersburg, Va., June 22, '64 and confined in the Libby, Bell Isle, and Andersonville Prisons, and died at the latter prison, Sept. 10, '64.

Henry T. Chalk,—Corp. of Company I. Enlisted July 5, 61; re-enlisted Dec. 11, '63; was captured near Milford, Va., May 28, '64, and confined in the Andersonville and Florence S. C. Prisons. Released, Feb. 28, '65, and discharged June 5, '65.

Henry B. Phipps,—Corp. of Co. C. Enlisted Aug. 15, '62; captured at Spottsylvania, Va., May 19, '64 and confined in the Andersonville Prison, where he died Aug. 24, '64.

John W. Chambers,—Private in Co. I. Enlisted Aug. 4, '62; was captured at Petersburg, Va., June 22 '64 and confined in the Libby, Va., Lynchburg, Va., Andersonville Ga. and Florence S. C. Prisons. Released—— Discharged, Feb. 1, '65.

Howard P. Gardner,—Private in Co. C. Enlisted Aug. 1, 62. Captured at Petersburg, Va., June 22 '64 and confined in the Andersonville, Ga. Prison; released——. Discharged, May, 17, '65.

John W. C. Avery,—Private in Co. G. Enlisted July 30, '62. Captured at Petersburg, Va., June 22, '64 and confined in the Libby, Belle Isle and Andersonville Prisons; he died at the latter, July 25, '64.

George H. Estes,—Private in Co. D. Enlisted July 29, '62. Captured June '64, and confined in the Andersonville Prison.

W. A. Smith,—Private in Co. D. Re-enlisted March 10, '64. Captured at Petersburg, Va., June 22, '64 and confined in the Libby, Belle Isle, Andersonville, Charleston and Florence Prisons. Released from Charleston, Dec. 16, '64; discharged, Aug. 16, '64.

Thomas Buxton,—Private in Co. G. Enlisted Aug. 5, '62. Captured at Petersburg, Va., June 22, '64, and confined in the Libby, Belle Isle and Andersonville Prisons. He died in the latter Aug. 5, '64.

Alfred Frye,—Private in Co. D. Enlisted July 30, '62; re-enlisted Dec. 31, 63. Captured and confined in the Andersonville Prison, where he died Dec. 26, '64.

John W. Mahoney,—Private in Co. D. Enlisted July 5, '61; re-enlisted Jan. 5, '64. Captured at Petersburg, Va, June 22, '64. Confined in the Libby, Belle Isle, Charleston, Florence and Andersonville Prisons; released at Wilmington, April 30, '65; discharged Aug. 16, '65.

Charles C. Wellman,—Private in Co. D. Enlisted Dec. 11, '63; was captured at Petersburg, Va., June 22, '64, and confined in the Libby, Belle Isle and Andersonville Prisons. He died Sept. 15, '64, in the latter Prison.

Robert C. Bassett,--Private in Co. I. Enlisted July 19, '62; was captured at Petersburg, June 22, '64, and confined in the Libby, Belle Isle and Andersonville Prisons. He died at the latter Prison Sept. 15, '64.

Patrick Buckley,—Private in Co. I. Enlisted July 5, '61; was captured at Petersburg, Va., June 22, '64, and confined in the Libby, Belle Isle, Andersonville, Charleston and Florence Prisons; released at Charleston in Dec. '64; discharged Jan. 25, '65.

Joseph H. Green,—Private in Co. I. Enlisted Aug. 6, '62; was captured at Petersburg, Va, June 22, '64, and confined in the Libby, Belle Isle, Andersonville, Florence and Charleston Prisons. He was released from the latter Dec. 1, '64, and died at Annapolis, Md., Dec. 10, '64.

Benjamin G. Helt,—Private in Co. I. Enlisted Aug. 5, '62; was captured at Petersburg, Va., June 22, '64, and confined in the Andersonville Prison; released Jan. 5, '65, and discharged March 15, '65.

Charles W. Coney,—Private in Co. L. Enlisted Feb. 28, '62; re-enlisted Feb. 29, '64; was captured at Petersburg, Va., June 22, '64, and confined in the Libby, Belle Isle and Andersonville Prisons. He died at the latter Prison, July 17, '64.

Samuel M. Fowler,—Corp. of Co. M. Enlisted March 20, '62; was captured at Petersburg, Va., June 22, '64; confined in Andersonville Prison, where he died Aug. 13, '64.

George W. Cross,—Private in Co. L. Enlisted Feb. 28, '62; re-enlisted Feb. 29, '64; was captured at Petersburg, Va., June 22, '64, and confined in the Libby, Belle Isle and Andersonville Prisons. He died at the latter Prison, July 17, '64.

Benjamin A. Phillips,—Private in Co. H. Enlisted Dec. 7, '63; was captured at Plymouth, N. C., April 20, '64, and confined in the Andersonville Prison; was released April 29, '65, at Baldwin, Fla.; discharged Aug. 14, '65.

John Savory,—Private in Co. H. Enlisted Dec. 9, '63; was captured at Plymouth, N.C., April 20, '64, and confined at Andersonville, Florence and Charleston Prisons. He died at the Florence Prison, Nov. 25, '64.

Twenty-Third Regiment Infantry, M.V.—Three Years.

Silas Winchester,—Corp. in Co. F. Enlisted Oct. 14, '62; captured at Drury's Bluff, May 16, '64. Confined in the Andersonville Prison, where he died.

Eli C. Thomas,—Private Co. F. Enlisted Oct. 4, '62; captured at Drury's Bluff, May 16, '64; confined in the Andersonville Prison, where he died Aug. 30, '64.

Twentieth Regiment Infantry, M.V.—Three Years.

Charles O. Newell,—Sergt. of Co. H. Enlisted Aug. 1, '61. Re-enlisted, Dec. 11, '63; captured at ———; confined in Libby and Salisbury Prisons; discharged, July 16, '65.

Nineteenth Regiment Infantry, M.V.—Three Years.

John Restelle jr.,—Private in Co. H. Enlisted, Dec. 10, '61; captured at White Oak Swamp Va., June 22, '62; released Aug. 10, '62; discharged, Dec. 20, '63; re-enlisted Dec. 21, and re-captured at Petersburg, Va., June 22, '64; confined in the Libby, Belle Isle, Miller, Ga., Andersonville and Castle Thunder, Va.; released Dec. 7, '64; discharged June 30, '65.

Ninth Regiment Infantry, M.V.—Three Years.

Patrick Sullivan,—Private in Co. F. Enlisted June 11, '61; captured, and confined in the Libby, Belle Isle and Andersonville Prisons. He died at the latter Prison, Sept. 18, '64.

Fifth Regiment Infantry, M.V.—Three Years.

Samuel A. Cate,—Private in Co. A. Enlisted May 1, '61; captured at Bull Run, July 21, '61, confined in the Libby Prison; released May 25, '62, and discharged June 24, '62.

William Shanley,—Private in Co. H. Enlisted May 1, '61; captured at Bull Run, July 21, '61; confined in Libby Prison; released and discharged in '62.

George W. Dow,—Private in Co. H. Enlisted, May 1, '61; captured at Bull Run, July 21, '61; confined in Libby Prison; released and discharged in '62.

Fourth Vermont Regiment Infantry,—Three Years.

John Day,—Private in Co. ———. Enlisted, ——— '61; captured ———; confined in the Libby Andersonville, Charleston and Florence Prisons; released and discharged '63.

MISCELLANEOUS.

Edwin Bailey,—Taken Prisoner at Cedar Mountain, Va., Aug. 9, '62.
George W. Langmaid,—Taken Prisoner in Banks' retreat May 25, '62.
Patrick Cusick,—Taken Prisoner at battle of Gaine's Mill, and confined in Richmond Prison.
Andrew L. Davis,—Private in Co. D. 1st Heavy Art. Taken Prisoner and escaped Feb. 26, '64; reported as deserted.
Andrew J. Blanchard.—Taken prisoner at Drury's Bluff, May 16, '64 and died in prison.
Peter Barrett,—Taken prisoner and died in prison, Feb. 16, '65.
George O. Hinckley,—Taken prisoner and died in Andersonville Prison, Sept. 6, '64.
Samuel H. Benson,—Taken prisoner, March 28, '65. Paroled March 29, '65.
Henry A. Bowler,—Co. C., 1st Reg. H. Art. Enlisted Aug. 4, '64. Taken prisoner and died in Andersonville Prison, Sept. 1, '64.
Dennis Leary,—Private in Co. A., 2d H. Art. Enlisted, July 28, '63. Taken prisoner and died at Andersonville, Ga., July 2, '64.
Jeremiah Lynch,—Private in Co. C., 22d Reg. Inf. Taken prisoner, and died in prison, Sept 15, '64.
Patrick Morgan,—Private, Co. B, 23d Reg. Inf. Taken prisoner and died at Andersonville, Ga., Sept. 7, '64.
William D. Parsons,—Private. Co. E. 23d Reg. Inf. Taken prisoner and died at Andersonville, Ga., June 22, '64.
Timothy Hart,—Private, Co. H. 20th Reg. Inf. Taken prisoner at Bull Run.
Abraham F. Warner,—Corp., Co. D, 19th Reg. Inf. Enlisted Feb. 16, '62. Taken prisoner and died at Andersonville, Ga., Nov. 23, '64.
John B. McKown,—Private, Co. F., 1st Heavy Art. Enlisted July 22, '61. Taken prisoner June 22, '64 and died at Malin, Ga., Nov. 18, '64.

KILLED IN THE SERVICE.

Allen Pickering D.—Killed at Brashear City, La., June 2, '63.
Bousley Theophilus F.—Killed in action at Port Hudson, June 12, '63.
Bancroft George C.—Killed at battle of Cold Harbor, June 1, '64.
Bateman Charles—Killed in action, Sept. 14, '63.
Brooks Richard—Killed June 30, '62.
Burns John—Killed at Williamsburg, Va , May 5, '62.
Batchelder George W.—Killed at Antietam, Md., Sept. 17, '62.
Cochran John—Supposed to have been killed at battle of Cedar Mountain, Va., Aug. 9, '62.
Casperson John P.—Killed in action, Sept. 17, '62.
Clark Sylvester—Killed in action at Little Washington, N. C., Sept. 19, '62.
Calaracan Charles—Killed at Laurel Hill, Va., May 10, '64.
Clark John A.—Killed at Wilderness, May 10, '64.
Dearborn Charles A. jr.—Killed at Fredericksburg, Dec. 30, '62.
Dalton Eleazer M. J.—Killed at Petersburg, June 22, '64.
Daley James—Killed at Culpepper, Va., Sept. 29, '63.
Derby Richard—Killed at Antietam, Md., Sept. 17, '62.
Emmerson Charles H.—Killed in action at Winchester, Va., while retreating through the town, May 25, '62.
Farrell Robert—Killed at battle Gaines Mill, June 27, '62.
Fleet George C.—Killed at battle of Petersburg, Va., June 22, '64.
Fowler William F.—Killed in action, Dec. 16, '62.
Francis Joseph—Killed at Battle of Wilderness, May, 26, '64.
Ganly John—Killed at battle of Malvern Hill, July 1, '62.
Gallnear Charles—Killed at battle of Laurel Hill, May 10, '64.
Guilford Samuel W.—Killed June 3, '64.
Gibbs William—Killed Nov. 30, '64.
Glover Henry B.—Killed at Williamsburg, Va., May 5, '62.
Hodges John jr., Col —Killed at Petersburg, Aug. 3, '64.
Hurley William—Killed, Sept 28, '64.
Hurrell John—Killed at Spottsylvania, Va., May 19, '64.
Hill Edwin R., 1st Lieut.—Killed in action, Dec. 9, '64.
Jewell Franklin—Killed in action at Cedar Mountain, Aug. 9, '62.
Keating Patrick—Killed at the battle of Chickihominey, June 27, '62.
Cole Robert—Killed in action at Natches' Run, May 20, '64.
Keenan Michael—Killed at Gaines Mill, Va., June 7, '62.
Larrabee William—Killed at battle of Cedar Mountain, Va., Aug. 19, '62.
Morrison John—Killed at Spottsylvania, Va., May 10, '64.
McNamara Peter—Killed at Gaines Mill, June 27, '62.
McGuire Patrick—Killed at the battle of Gaines Mill, June 27, '62.
Morrissey John—Killed at the battle of Fredericksburg, Dec. 13, '63.
Musgrave Peter—Killed at Petersburg, Va , June 16, '64.
Mc Mahon John—Killed in action, May 12, '64.
Martin George A.—Killed at Petersburg, Va., Feb 27, '65.
Murphy Luke—Killed June 25, '62.
Merritt Henry—Killed at battle of Newbern, N. C , March 14, '62.
Mullen Patrick A.—Killed Aug. 14, '64,
McCarthy John—Drowned in Mississippi River, Sept. 6, '64
McMahon James—Killed at Gaines Mill, Va., June 27, '62.
Moran James—Killed at Bull Run, Va., Aug. 29, '62.
McKenzie John W.—Killed at Spottsylvania, Va., May 10, '64.
Neil Edward—Killed at Gaines Mill, Va., June 27, '62.
Noyes Edward D.--Killed at Fredericksburg, Va , Dec 13, '62.
Osgood Cyrus M.—Killed at Fredericksburg, May 1, '63.
O'Connell Timothy—Killed at Blanford, Va., June 19, '64.
Powers James—Killed at battle of Shady Grove, Va., June 31, '62.
Parsons George W —Killed in action, Oct. 2, '64.
Pulsifer David F.—Killed in action at Kingston, N. C. March 28, '65.
Plummer David—Killed in action, Aug. 13, '62.
Purbeck William L.—Killed at Gettysburg, Penn., July 2, '63

Preston John F.—Killed at Wilderness, Va., May 6, '64.
Regan James—Killed at battle of Gaines Mill, Va., June 27, '62.
Ross William H.—Killed in action, at Spottsylvania, Va , May 10, '64.
Staples George—Killed at Winchester, May 26, '62.
Sullivan Patrick—Killed near Richmond, Va., July 1, '62.
Staples Elias C.—Killed near Spottsylvania, Va., May 17, '64.
Smith William J.—Killed at Fredericksburg, Va., May 3, '63.
Swaney William H.—Killed in action at Drury's Bluff, May 6, '64.
Short Joseph A.—Killed at White Oak Swamp, June 29, '62.
Saunders John—Killed in action, Sept. 17, '62.
Swasey William R.—Killed at battle of Bull Run, Va., Aug. 29, '62.
Stillman Samuel—Killed at Laurel Hill, Va., May 8, '64.
Thompson George A.—Killed at battle of Bull Run, July 21, '61.
Vaughan Charles—Killed May 13. '64.
Williston William H.—Killed at battle of Cedar Mountain, Aug. 9, '62.
Wilkins George G.—Killed May 16, '64.
Ward Charles G.—Killed at Drury's Bluff, May 16, '64.
Webb Augustine—Killed at Fort, Charleston Harbor, Aug. 20, '63.
Wiley George, 1st Sergt.—Killed July 30, '64.
Welch John—Killed at Winchester, Va., Sept. 19, '64.

DIED IN THE SERVICE.

Alton Samuel S—Died July 19, '64.
Allen Benjamin—Died of wounds, Aug. 30, '64.
Ashbell Wyatt—Died of disease, Sept. 24, '63.
Austin Alden K.—Died at Newbern, N. C., Oct. 12, '64.
Avery John W. C.—Died at Andersonville, Ga., July 25, '64.
Alton Samuel T.—Died at Gettysburg, Pa., July 17, '63.
Bradley John—Died of wounds at Salem, June 20, '64.
Bassett Robert C.—Died at Andersonville, Sept. 15, '64.
Barnes John—Died of wounds, May 8, '62.
Brown John B.—Died at Yorktown, Va., July 8, '62.
Byrns George W.—Died of wounds, Nov. 2, '62.
Brown George A.—Died of wounds, Dec. 17, '62.
Blanchard Andrew J.—Died in Rebel Prison, Nov. 11, '64.
Brooks Samuel H.—Died of wounds received at Newbern, N. C., April 6, '62.
Brown Augustus—Died at Newbern, N. C., Sept. 22, '62.
Barrett Peter—Died in Rebel Prison, Feb. 16, '65.
Butman George A.—Died of disease, May 28, '64.
Bodwell John A.—Died at Newport News, Va., Aug. 20, '62.
Barnes Israel D.—Died May 6, '65.
Barnard Samuel—Died at Fort Pike, La., Nov. 13, '62.
Boyce John F.—Died at Fort Pike, La., Nov. 11, '62.
Buxton Seth G.—Died Jan. 15, '63.
Bowler Henry A.—Died at Andersonville, Ga., Sept. 1, '64.
Buxton Thomas—Died at Andersonville, Ga., Aug. 5, '64.
Cross George W.—Died in Andersonville Prison, July 27, '64.
Carey James—Died Oct. 25, '62.
Cahill Bartholomew—Died at Dangerfield Hospital, Va., Jan. 22, '65.
Coggwell Epes—Died at Fort Pike, La., Nov. 12, '62.
Cowee George L.—Died at New Orleans, La., Oct. 23, '62.
Coney Charles W.—Died at Andersonville, Ga., Aug. 8, '64.
Crowley Philip—Died at Carrolton, La., Aug. 24, '62.
Chandler Isaac H.—Died of wounds, May 14, '64.
Dodge Joseph R.—Died at Port Hudson, July 26, '63.
Davis James B.—Died at N O., Oct. 28, '62.
Donahoe Thomas—Died at N. O., Nov. 13, '62.
Dodge Joseph H.—Died at Fort Delaware, Sept. 15, '64.
Dresser Charles F.—Died at City Point, Nov. 15, '64.
Edwards George W.—Died, Sept. 29, '62.
Findley Edward—Died at Baton Rouge, La., Feb. 23, '63.
Foster Patrick— Died of disease, Feb. 21, '63.
Frothingham John P.—Died of wounds, June 16, '64, received at Petersburg, Va.
Frye Alfred—Died a prisoner at Andersonville, Ga., Dec. 26, '64.
Fowler Samuel W.—Died at Andersonville, June 22, '64.
Fish Charles W.—Died
Friend Alfred—Died of wounds, received at James Island, July 17, '63.
Flakefield Charles—Died at Kingston N. C. of wounds.
Fabens William P.—Died at Fort Wagner, Aug. 30, '64.
Foot Moses F.—Died at N. Orleans, Oct. 28, '62
Farmer George S.—Died at Andersonville, Ga., Sept. 10, '64.
Frothingham Gustavus—Died at Petersburg, Va., June 24, '64.
Gillon Hugh—Died at Fortress Munroe.
Getchell Charles L.—Died at Newbern, N. C., April 9, '62.
Greenough John W. jr.—Died of wounds, June 26, '64.
Gwinn Edward—Died of wounds, June 19, '64.
Green Joseph H.—Died at Annapolis, Md., Dec. 20, 64
Gifford Frank—Died at Hampton, Va., June 29, '64.
Gifford Charles P.—Died, July 1, '62.
Hinkley George O.—Died in Rebel Prison about Oct. '64.
Hassett Martin—Died July 13, '63.

Hayse Maurice—Died at Baton Rouge, La., Aug. 9, '62.
Helpin James—Died April 13, '65.
Hogan James—Died of wounds received at Wilderness, May 18, '64.
Hart Joseph L.—Died at Fort Pike La., Dec. 1, '62.
Hurley William—Died at Arlington, Va., Sept. 17, '64.
Haskell Charles—Died at Salem, March 10, '64.
Harrington Daniel—Died of wounds, March 27, '65.
Ingalls John—Died near Falmouth, Va., Feb. 17, '63.
Knowlton George—Died at Baton Rouge, La., April 7, '63.
Keenan Michael—Died June 27, '62.
Kinsman Joseph N.—Died Oct. 17, '64.
Kezar Albert—Died at Salem, Nov. 1, '62.
Kittredge Henry A.—Died Oct. 9, '62.
Lightfoot Joseph—Died of wounds, Sept. 19, '64.
Leighton William—Died March 26, '63.
Leary Dennis—Died at Andersonville, July 2, '64.
Lynch Jeremiah—Died at Rebel Prison, Sept. 15, '64.
Manning Horace—Died at Fort DeKalb, June 13, '64.
McKonn John B.—Died at Milan, Ga., Nov. 18, '64.
McNamara Michael—Died, Oct. 15, '62.
McIntire George—Died of wounds, received at Newbern, April 10, '62.
Masury Thomas A.—Died of wounds, Feb. 6, '63.
McFarland Peter—Died Dec. 20, '63.
McCabe Patrick—Died at Salem, July 28, '64.
Manning David A.—Died at N. Orleans, La., Oct. 28, '64.
Maquer John—Died at Galveston, Texas, July 3, '65.
Melley W. I—Died at N. Orleans, La., Feb. 11, '63.
Munroe George—Died at New Orleans, La. Aug. 31, '62.
Morgan Patrick—Died at Andersonville, Sept. 6, '64.
McGordis Charles—Died of wounds at City Point, June 24, '64.
Mathews Lawrence—Died of wounds at Wilderness, May 6, '64.
Millett Daniel S.—Died at Gettysburg, Pa., July 13, '63.
Maxwell Silas—Died at Newbern, N. C., Sept. 1, '62.
Mc Donald David—Died at Alexandria, Va., Aug. 25, '64.
Nolan Thomas—Died at Memphis, Jan. 8, '65.
Ober Oliver—Died at Mound City, Aug. '63.
Oldson Francis T.—Died of wounds, Sept. 6, '62.
Preston Otis P.—Died at Baton Rouge, La., May 26, '63.
Penderghast Thomas—Died at Salem, May 20, '65.
Parsons William D.—Died at Andersonville, Ga., June 22, '64.
Pinkham William A.—Died Sept. 30, '64.
Peckham Charles—Died at Fort Warren, May 21, '64.
Pinkham Charles—Died at Fort Warren, May 21, '64.
Pulsifer Nathaniel F.—Died of disease at Fairfax Hospital, Nov. 29, '64.
Phipps Henry B.—Died at Andersonville, Ga., Aug. 26, '64.
Pitman Nathaniel F.—Died of wounds at Washington, D. C., Sept. 12, '64.
Potter Francis B.—Died at Washington, D. C., June 5, '64.
Phippen Abraham—Died at Greebon, N. C., June 18, '65.
Prince George—Died of wounds at Port Lookout, Md., June 9, '64.
Redmond Philip E.—Died at Washington, D. C., Sept. 11, '65.
Regan Edmund—Died of wounds received at Malvern Hill, Sept. 16, '62.
Rogan William—Died at Long Island, Boston Harbor.
Reeves William H.—Died at Fort Albany, Va., Dec. 1, '61.
Regan Michael—Died at Beverly Hospital, N. Y., Oct. 29, '64.
Roberts George—Died of wounds, Feb. 6, '65.
Rowe James H.—Died Nov. 8, '64.
Ricker James—Died at Salem, of wounds, Aug. 26, '62.
Rogers Simon A.—Died at Fort Warren, April 6, '65.
Rodwell John A.—Died at Port News, Va., Aug. 20, '62.
Stratton Benjamin F.—Died at Baton Rouge, La., May 1, '63.
Simon John F.—Died at Baton Rouge, La. April 18, '63.
Smith Patrick—Died at Salem, Dec. 10, '62
Shea Patrick—Died of wounds, received at Savage Station, May 31, '64.
Sherlock Thomas S.—Died of disease at Bealton Station, Feb. '64.
Snell Nicholas T.—Died at Salem of wounds received in action, May 24, '62.

Stillman Samuel—Died March 27, '63.
Schultz Carl F.—Died at Newbern, N. C., April 24, '64.
Savory John—Died at Florence, S. C., Dec. 25, '64.
Simmons William—Died at Salem, Feb 9, '65.
Stover Nathaniel F.—Died at Salem, May 16, '64.
Sullivan Patrick—Died at Andersonville, Ga., Sept. 18, '64.
Shaw Orlin—Died of wounds, at Gettysburg, Pa., Aug. 3, '62.
Saunders Henry T.—Died at Newbern, N. C.. Oct. 9, '64.
Trofater Elias A.—Died on board Gunboat Omaha, July 30, '63.
Tracy John—Died at Philadelphia, Pa.
Tarbox Randall—Died at Harrison's Landing, Va., Aug. 15, '62.
Towne Calvin E.--Died at Lincoln General Hospital, Oct. 8, '64.
Thomas James—Died Oct. 13, '64.
Thomas Eli C.—Died in Rebel Prison, Aug. 30, '64.
Townsend William H.—Died July 2, '64.
Thompson Franklin B.—Died at New Orleans, July 29, '62.
Trull Charles W.—Died at Fort Pike, La., Nov. 11, '62.
Tufts John A.—Died at New Orleans, La.
Thrasher Nathaniel—Died at Memphis, Ten., April 8, '65.
Waters James V.—Died on board transport, Omaha, Aug. 63.
Wallace John A.—Died at Fredericksburg, Va., April 9, '62.
Winters Lawrence—Died at Falmouth, Va., Sept. 6, '62.
Wheeler Michael—Died at Washington, D. C., Aug. 1, '64.
Wheeler Richard T.—Died of wounds received at Drury's Bluff, June 21, '64.
Warner William W.—Died at Sea, July 14, '64.
Williams Charles F.—Died of wounds, Dec. 22, '62.
Wentworth John H.—Died at New Orleans, La., May 26, '62.
Williams William D.—Died at New Orleans, La., March 26, '63.
Welch Michael—Died at Cairo, Ill., Jan. 16, '65.
Warner Abraham—Died at Andersonville, Ga., Nov. 23, '64.
Warner George L.—Died at Belil, Va., Oct. 18, '62.

J. PERLEY,
BOOK-BINDER,
AND
BLANK BOOK
MANUFACTURER,
NO. 2 ST. PETER STREET,
SALEM, MASS.

PERIODICALS, OF ALL DESCRIPTIONS,

Bound in Plain and Ornamental Style.

—

PAPER RULED,

And Blank Books made to any desired Pattern.

R. A. MACKENZIE,
Merchant Tailor.

A FULL LINE OF CLOTHS,

CASSIMERES AND VESTINGS,

CONSTANTLY ON HAND.

Reasonable Prices and satisfaction guaranteed.

287 ESSEX STREET,

SALEM, MASS.

LADIES' NOTICE.

Millinery Goods.

The Latest Shades and Shapes can always be found at
J. H. BROWNE'S
Magazine de la Mode,
155 ESSEX STREET, SALEM.

Hats and Bonnets trimmed to order at short notice.
Crape Work, all kinds at low prices.
ALSO, REAL HAIR GOODS, SWITCH BRAIDS, CURLS, &c.
KID GLOVES CLEANSED AT ONE DAY'S NOTICE.

ORDERS BY MAIL PROMPTLY ATTENDED TO.

155 Essex Street, next door to the Museum.

Day's Popular Boot & Shoe Shop,

12 1-2 LAFAYETTE STREET,

NEAR THE BRIDGE, SALEM.

It is now one year since I opened this repair shop, and put out the first bulletin board ever shown in New England, advertising prices for repairing. My trade is now very large and I am obliged to employ extra help, and the secret of my success is simply because I have always done just as I agreed.

1st. To always have work out at the hour promised.
2d. Because my work always is warranted and has always proved just as represented.

Considering the extreme dull, hard times, I have made some reductions in my prices which are as follows.

Fine and Heavy Boots and Shoes, half soled and heeled, and every pair warranted, $1 00
"   "   "   "   "   "   fair work and stock, 80

Ladies' Nobby high heels, 20 cents.
Ladies' Boots and Slippers, half soled and heeled, 65 cents.
Boys' Boots and Shoes, half soled and heeled, best of stock and work, 75 cents.
Misses' and Children's Shoes and Slippers, half soled and heeled, 25 to 45 cents.
All kinds of Rubber wear, half soled and heeled, or patched at short notice.
Men's Second Hand Boots and Shoes constantly on hand and sold cheap for cash.

Hoping to merit a continuance of your patronage,
I am Respectfully,

JOHN DAY,
12 1-2 LAFAYETTE STREET, SALEM.

J. W. AYERS,

Manufacturer of Artistic Furniture. Upholstering in all its branches. 8 1-2 and 10 1-2 Lafayette Street, Salem.

A. G. SWETT,

Dealer in Boots, Shoes and Rubbers, at low prices. 9 Lafayette Street, Salem.

CASSINO & GARDNER,

Dealers in Pictures Frames, Chromos, Engravings, &c. Reguilding a Specialty 273 Essex Street, Salem.

A. M. NEAL & CO.,

Dealers in Picture Frames, Chromos, Engravings, Blank Books, Stationery, &c., &c. 144 Essex Street, Salem.

WARREN PORTER, D. D. S.,

Dentistry in all its branches. 237 Essex Street, Salem.

www.ingramcontent.com/pod-product-compliance
Lightning Source LLC
Chambersburg PA
CBHW020108170426
43199CB00009B/452